THE GOSPEL According To JONAH

JUSTIN DEAN

LUCIDBOOKS

The Gospel According to Jonah

Published by Lucid Books in Houston, TX.
www.LucidBooks.net

All scripture quotations, unless otherwise indicated, are taken from the Holy Bible, English Standard Version (ESV).

First Printing 2015

ISBN 10: 1632960621
ISBN 13: 978-1-63296-062-7

eISBN 10: 163296063X
eISBN 13: 978-1-63296-063-4

TABLE OF CONTENTS

INTRODUCTION

I doubt you are opening this book for a detailed description of the insides of a whale. If that's what you are looking for, you can toss this book now and do a quick Google search to satisfy that fancy. It's my guess that you are probably already moderately familiar with this ancient story of Jonah and the whale. It is a fantastic story, but is it fantasy? Surprisingly, Jesus said no. Or at least He implied as much when He used the story of Jonah's time in the belly of the whale as an analogy of His time spent in a borrowed rich man's tomb (Matthew 12:40). And it's this discovery that makes the story of Jonah so complex. After Jesus was crucified and resurrected, the Gospel of Luke tells us that Jesus came back and spent time with His disciples. Apparently, the flesh and blood resurrection of Jesus was so unexpected that even Jesus' closest followers had given up hope and went on with their lives. Jesus returned to reassure them that He was indeed the Christ, the long-awaited King who would heal all of creation, but He also appeared to them to change the way they read the Old Testament, including the book of Jonah. This is how Luke describes it in his Gospel:

> And he said to them, "O foolish ones, and slow of heart to believe all that the prophets have spoken! Was it not necessary that the Christ should suffer these things and enter into his glory?" And beginning with Moses and all the Prophets, he interpreted to them in all the Scriptures the things concerning himself (Luke 24:25-27).

This passage shows us that Jesus is giving His followers a new way of seeing and reading the Old Testament, a Christ-centered way. Jesus is saying that the entire Old Testament, from Genesis to Malachi, is all about Him. That means in our study of the book of Jonah we have at least two layers of consideration. We have the factual layer, that is, the historical account and context. Jonah involves real people in real places in history—it actually happened. But we also have the Christ-centered layer. Everything that happened in Jonah was "concerning Jesus." It points to Jesus, it centers on Jesus, and it prefigures Jesus in ways that Jonah was not aware of at the time. So as we read this book, we will use these two layers of interpretation as two lenses to take a deeper look into this familiar story. What we will find is nothing short of life-changing.

The book of Jonah is about a man on the run from God, and the lengths to which the God of the Bible will go to love such men and women. I have been such a man. I am often such a man still, and every time I come back to this story I am overwhelmed at the reckless love of God that pursues people on the run. If you have ever been tempted to run from this God, or maybe you are on the run right now, my prayer for you would be to take a fresh look at this story and let it reveal to you the heart of the God who chases us down, not to punish us, but to love us with a love so steadfast that the word salvation best describes it. This is the gospel according to Jonah.

THE RUNNING MAN

Now the word of the LORD came to Jonah the son of Amittai, saying, "Arise, go to Nineveh, that great city, and call out against it, for their evil has come up before me." But Jonah rose to flee to Tarshish from the presence of the LORD. He went down to Joppa and found a ship going to Tarshish. So he paid the fare and went down into it, to go with them to Tarshish, away from the presence of the LORD.

But the LORD hurled a great wind upon the sea, and there was a mighty tempest on the sea, so that the ship threatened to break up. Then the mariners were afraid, and each cried out to his god. And they hurled the cargo that was in the ship into the sea to lighten it for them. But Jonah had gone down into the inner part of the ship and had lain down and was fast asleep. So the captain came and said to him, "What do you mean, you sleeper? Arise, call out to your god! Perhaps the god will give a thought to us, that we may not perish."

And they said to one another, "Come, let us cast lots, that we may know on whose account this evil has come upon us." So they cast lots, and the lot fell on Jonah. Then they said to him, "Tell us on whose account this evil has come upon us. What is your occupation? And where do you come from? What is your country? And of what people are you?" And he said to them, "I am a Hebrew, and I fear the LORD, the God of heaven, who made the sea and the dry land." Then the men were exceedingly afraid and said to him, "What is this that you have done!" For the men knew that he was fleeing from the presence of the LORD, because he had told them.

—Jonah 1:1-10

Despite being one of the best-known stories in the entire Bible, the book of Jonah is often tragically misunderstood. Everyone knows about the fish, right? Sure, we love the big fish. It makes for great kid stories! But very few people really know that this book is all about man running from God, and God chasing after man. There is a fish involved, but mainly it is about man running from God while God graciously pursues man with His one-way love.

This is the core message of Christianity in story form, and I believe it meets our deepest need as people. We need to rediscover this story today. We need it because we have become hardened to it, blind to it, and the warmth of it doesn't affect our heart the way it should. We end up like Jonah, running from grace. When we rediscover this story, it changes us—not just our theology, but also our hearts. It enables us to love God and love others in a greater way.

For me, this happened about six years ago, and it came through a very difficult season of life. I felt called to plant a church, but when I decided to start this new church, I was fired from my job as a youth pastor. I didn't know what to do, and I felt as if my life were in a storm and turned upside down. How was I going to start a church with no money, no support, and no idea what I was doing? On top of everything my wife was eight months pregnant with our second child. Up until that moment I hadn't realized that my life was built upon my performance. It was built upon my achievement, hard work, and effort. I was preaching the gospel but at the same time I didn't get it in my soul. I kind of knew it in my head, but I wasn't humble or broken by it. I didn't see my own sin very well—I was proud of our ministry. I had created a youth ministry from seven teenagers (four of which were my family members) and had grown it in seven years to a gathering of well over 300 students each week. We were sending dozens of missionaries overseas, we had started a local nonprofit coffee shop whose full proceeds went to Costa Rican orphans, and we had just adopted around 70 Kenyan orphans for monthly support.

Through the gospel and difficult circumstances, God changed the type of man I am, the type of father I am, the type of husband I am, the type of pastor I am, and the type of church planter I am. Sacred City Church (the church I eventually planted) is the result of God changing my heart. If I had planted this church six years before, the church would have been an extension of my ego and would have been all about the Sunday Gathering, about looking slick and polished. But God changed my heart, and that change spilled over into our church and has changed the hearts of a couple hundred people who call Sacred City home. I hope this happens to many people through this book. I hope that the gospel will travel from these pages into hearts and really change the type of people we are so that we can love God and love others in a more heartfelt way. I think the book of Jonah is going to help us accomplish that purpose, because the book of Jonah tells a gospel story that is just shocking enough to wake us up to grace.

Many of us have heard the word "grace" (you might have some kind of working definition of it), but Jonah is going to show us that our primary problem in life is that we run from the

God of grace because we actually do not like grace. If God feels distant to you, that is because—and, you might not even know it—you are running from grace. That is why you walk around with this sense in yourself that something isn't right. Perhaps somehow you have this vague sense that God is not pleased with you and you need to do something to fix it. You might feel there is always this responsibility on you to do something—shape up, be better, or do more. There is this "thing" on you, this nagging sense that makes you wonder "am I good enough for God?"

If we feel that God is disappointed with us all of the time, why would we want to come to a church gathering? Why would we want to come near to God? Why would we want to be near Him if all that being near Him does is make us feel worthless, broken, and confirms all the doubts we have about ourselves?

In his book *Surprised by Joy*, C.S Lewis says (and our culture says this kind of stuff a lot), "Amiable agnostics will talk cheerfully about 'man's search for God.' To me, as I then was, they might as well have talked about the mouse's search for a cat."[1] Why would a mouse go looking for a cat? That's mouse suicide! So, when preachers get up in the pulpit and we tell you that you should love God—LOVE GOD—not just obey Him, not just bend to His will, but *love Him*—those are two contrasting things! How can I love a God that I am too afraid to be near? How can I love a God who, when I am near Him, just confirms all the bad things that I think about myself?

That's what Jonah is all about—that nagging sense that we all have of not being good enough. We think we need something else in our lives. "I just need a little bit more money." "I just need that promotion." "I just need one more child." It's that nagging sense, the awareness that you are somehow broken, you are somehow lacking. You just need one more thing to push you over the top into happiness, into satisfaction. It's that distance you feel between you and God (He's cold, distant, far away) even when you are surrounded by a room full of people. You still feel distant; you still feel lonely. The Bible has a word for that. It's called *sin.*

That word has completely fallen out of vogue (if it ever was in vogue) in our society. You will never turn on the news and hear them talk about sin, but what's interesting is that we all still feel like sinners. So, now we have this quandary in our culture: we all feel messed up, but our culture doesn't even have a word to describe what is wrong with us. If our culture can't describe what is wrong with us, then of course it doesn't have any answers for us!

So what does our culture do? We create false problems to solve through consumerism. The other day while I was watching football with my son, he said, "Dad, what's the point of commercials?"

I said, "It's easy, son, to make you unhappy."

"What?"

"That's the point of commercials. They are going to make you unhappy with your current circumstances and then convince you that happiness is found on the other side of purchasing their product. They created a problem, then solved it with their product. I'm not happy unless I have a phone as big as my Bible, or unless I have those clothes, or unless I vote for that person. I don't think that stuff is going to work though."

Here's the good thing about having a label for what is actually wrong with us and about understanding what sin is: if you have the diagnosis, you can also get a prescription for it. My wife, in her last month of pregnancy, was having weird back pains that were very frustrating for us. She would wake up in the middle of the night in a lot of pain. People would say, "Oh, it's back labor," or "Oh, it's kidney stones," but nobody knew what the heck was going on. This is why we need the Bible; this is why we need God. There's something wrong with us, and the Bible clearly says what it is. When God diagnoses it, He also gives the prescription for it: *the grace, mercy, and kindness of God seen in the gospel of Jesus Christ.*

Now, when I say the word "sin," there is a lot of baggage behind that word. Everybody thinks we don't need to talk about sin because everybody already knows what it is. I don't think everybody knows what sin is. I think we all have our ideas and concepts of what sin is, but we actually need to be shocked by a biblical perspective of it. If you are non-religious and grew up in a secular home, or if you grew up outside of a faith community, you'd probably say that sin is breaking the rules—actually, you might say that sin is breaking all the rules keeping you from fun, because that is how it looks from outside the church! You might consider sin to be breaking some arbitrary rules set by the Bible or society or something else. Contrast that definition of sin with a religious person.

Religious people's concept of sin is funny. Religious people's concept of sin is what they used to do, or what their neighbor does, or what people on the news do, or what those people in that other part of town do. They see it as the "really bad" things they might have dabbled in when they were younger. This kind of thinking makes religious people really hesitant to hang around with the type of people who would blatantly sin in those ways. It makes religious people really distant to those who are suffering. It makes religious people really cold and hard and even blind to their own sin and their own inadequacies. They come off as proud and cold and looking down on those who don't sin in the same way that they do. And when religious people begin to look down on others, their hearts get cold and distant toward God. They don't know it, but they are distant from Him because they are trying to relate to God through their own ideas of morality instead of grace, and grace is the only way that God relates to a sinful human race.

However, knowing you are a sinner doesn't fix anything. It's just the diagnosis, right? Knowing you "used to be a sinner and now you're trying really hard not to be" doesn't help you very much either. What we must see (and Jonah shows us) are the specific ways that we run from God. Right now, I believe, many if not all of us are actively running away from God and His grace. We need to see how we are running away from Him, we need to confess it to Him, and we need to allow the aggressive grace of God to overtake us and lavish us with His one-way love. That is what we need, yet with full awareness that we don't deserve it. That is what is going to change us into people who love God and others with a soft-hearted reckless abandon that has the ability to change our homes, neighborhoods, cities, and even the world.

But like a wave in the ocean, the grace of God doesn't come to us nice and neatly; it doesn't come to us on our own terms. The grace of God overwhelms us, shocks us, and levels us. It comes no other way. So as we start this journey together, let us ask God to speak to us from this old story about a man named Jonah.

Now the word of the LORD came to Jonah the son of Amittai, saying, "Arise, go to Nineveh, that great city, and call out against it, for their evil has come up before me." (1:1-2)

This story starts like many Old Testament prophetic books with the phrase "the word of the Lord" or more accurately "the word of Yahweh (YHWH)." So, the God of Israel, the God of the Hebrew people, comes to this guy named Jonah. The books of Jeremiah, Isaiah, Joel, and Hosea all ring out with this phrase. Whenever you see this unique Hebrew phrase in the Bible, know that it is specific to the calling or functioning of a prophet.

Jonah was a prophet. He was chosen by God to be God's

mouthpiece, to speak the word of God to the people of God. This was his calling, his vocation, his God-given identity. As we keep reading, verse 3 brings a big plot twist:

> **Now the word of the LORD came to Jonah the son of Amittai, saying, "Arise, go to Nineveh, that great city, and call out against it, for their evil has come up before me." But Jonah rose to flee to Tarshish from the presence of the LORD. (1:1-3)**

Here is the first major plot twist in the book. Jonah, God's man, God's preacher, God's prophet, hears the word of the Lord and then turns and runs in the opposite direction.

Jonah is going to show us what sin does and how sin creeps in. Sin is not just breaking the rules; it's worse than that. Jonah isn't just breaking the rules; it's worse than that. Jonah is committing identity suicide! Jonah essentially tells God, "I don't want to be Your prophet anymore. I don't want the identity You have given me. You have called me to be a prophet and I don't want it anymore. Here, You can have it back. I'd rather go my own way, do my own thing, build my own identity. No thanks, God! I'll build my own life on my own rules."

Sin is far more than just disobeying the rules. Sin is trying to build your identity on anything other than God. When you try to do this—when you build the center of who you are on something other than God Himself—nothing but trouble is ahead of you. Your identity will be too weak; it won't be strong enough to weather the storms of your life. You will have an identity implosion or explosion sometime in your life. And this is what happened to Jonah.

> **"Arise, go to Nineveh, that great city, and call out against it, for their evil has come up before me." (1:2)**

At this time, Nineveh was the biggest, baddest, most dominant city in the world. Approximately 750 years before the birth of Jesus Christ, Nineveh was the capital city of Assyria, which is modern day Iraq. The remains of this great city lie just across the river from Mosul. For us to understand what is going on with Jonah, we need to dig down into the context a little bit.

Assyria was an imperialistic nation that was taking over the surrounding nations, and Israel was next on their hit list and knew at any moment that they could be taken over. Assyria was a sworn enemy of Israel. So, when the word of the Lord comes to Jonah and tells him to go to Nineveh, it's about as welcome as if God were to tell us to go preach to the Islamic State in Iraq.

We would probably not welcome that message. God says, "Go tell that pagan, powerful city to repent." It sounds like some old preachers I heard when I was growing up. You go tell them good-for-nothing, rotten sinners that God's coming to get 'em. Judgment's coming!

But, look at this plot twist! Nineveh is evil and disobedient. They're sinful; *but so is Jonah!* God's own prophet, God's preacher, gets his marching orders and then goes in the completely opposite direction. Now it's easy for us to think, "That's a tough job! Go to Iraq and preach to IS? You are going to get killed. You'll be beheaded." But that is not why Jonah turns and goes the opposite direction, not at all. This book is full of surprises! We don't find out completely until Chapter 4, but I will give you a heads up.

Jonah's reason for fleeing isn't that he's afraid of getting beheaded by the Assyrians. Instead, Jonah knows God; he knows God's character and nature. Jonah doesn't want to go because he knows that God is merciful, gracious, slow to anger, and abounding in steadfast love.

Jonah runs from God because he is afraid that he might be successful! He's afraid that he'll declare the word of the LORD to the Ninevites, they will actually turn away from their sin, and then God will graciously invite them into the family of God! Jonah is repelled by the grace of God! He just cannot believe that God would take these no-good sinners and invite them into His family.

Jonah runs in the opposite direction instead of preaching to the Ninevites because he is afraid that God would grant them repentance. I started out this book saying that we all run from grace. That's our problem. That's why we feel far from God. That's why we struggle to forgive those who have hurt us, and why we think we need more and more and more money. We are running from the very thing that will satisfy our souls. We are running from the cure: the all-satisfying grace of God. We run from the idea that God could actually love us just as we are! That He could really be into us even though we are so inadequate! We don't believe it could really be true.

Jonah is going to show us that we are wrong. Through this story we will see that there are two predominant ways that we run from this gracious God.

One way that we run is evident through the Assyrians, the Ninevites. They run from the grace of God through outright rebellion. This is liberalism; this is where people throw off all restraints. "I am my own God. I make my own rules. I determine what is right and wrong for myself. Who is God to tell me how to live my life?" This is one way people run from grace: the liberal route.

But, we also see here a different route and one much more dangerous. Why is it more dangerous? Because it's covert. This way to run from grace flies under the radar of most people's morality. It's like the stealth bomber of sin—it's almost undetectable until it's too late and right on top of you. Then, your whole life comes apart, your identity is gone, and you don't know what to do. Jonah runs from grace through his religious, moral, and cultural pride. This is moralism. It's interesting that here in the book of Jonah, when you look at all four chapters, the "bad guy" is actually the "good guy"—the true rebel is the rule follower! God's prophet is actually the "big sinner" in this book who is running from grace and running from God as fast as his feet can take him! In this story, it's the religious moral conservative that is the true outlaw running from God.

Why in the heck is Jonah running? Why is Jonah so afraid that these people are going to get grace and are going to be adopted into God's gracious family? II Kings 14:25 tells us that Jonah prophesied to Israel during a time of unparalleled prosperity. Israel was expanding their borders back to the size they were when David was king. Things were going well for Israel—which doesn't happen very often if you know the history of the nation of Israel. So, Jonah is on the winning team, something very few prophets got to do. Ezekiel's job was basically to tell Israel to quit being whores! He said over and over again, "You are whoring yourself out to other nations." Jeremiah also had a bad rep—he was the weeping prophet who wept all the time because his job was so hard. Jonah, on the other hand, was one of the only prophets who actually had a good job for most of his life. He preached during a time of expansion and prosperity.

Everybody likes that prophet. But now, in the midst of this cultural expansion, in the midst of Israel being built up, God turns Jonah toward Nineveh. God essentially tells Jonah, "Your enemy over there, Assyria, the one threatening you? The one you are afraid is going to carry you off into slavery? Go preach to them. Go tell them that I am a good, gracious, loving God, and if they turn from their sin, they can be adopted into my family." But Jonah isn't interested in that at all.

To put it simply, Jonah is racist. Jonah wants God to be the

God of Israel and Israel alone. He doesn't want these godless, rebellious pagans from Nineveh to get grace. He wants to be in God's inner ring. You know what the "inner ring" is, right? It's that one lunch table in junior high—you know the one—or the football huddle, or the sorority. Everybody wants to be in the inner ring somewhere. We all want to be accepted and known and loved by those in that inner ring. We all want to feel like insiders, and Jonah was no different.

The thing about inner rings, though, is that they don't exist unless there are others on the outside. If you make your way to *that* lunch table, then you get to look around and scoff at all the peasants at other tables, right? Jonah wants to be in God's inner ring. He doesn't want these outsiders to be grafted in. Being an Israelite is more important to his identity than being forgiven as one of God's people through grace.

See, Jonah has an immature concept of sin. But the truth is, whether we like it or not, we are just like him. We view the world like an old western made up of good guys and bad guys. All the bad guys come in wearing black hats, and all the good guys come in wearing white hats. Right away you can tell who the good guys are and who the bad guys are, and depending on your personality, you can pick up a hat. You want to be a bad guy? Grab a black hat. Want to be a good guy? Grab a white hat. This is how Jonah sees the world: Ninevites wear black hats; Israelites wear white hats.

In this system we believe that God actually loves the good guys and is opposed to and hates the bad guys—*thankfully, of course, we are one of the good guys*. Isn't that how we always see ourselves? It's always the opposing political group that is trying to destroy America. We get a lot of this in the news right now. They are like Nazis in disguise trying to tank our country. It's not only that they hold opposing ideas, but it's also that "they're wicked!" We want to throw a label on people so we don't have to love them or be friends with them. There are no insiders without outsiders. This is how Jonah views the Ninevites: *they are what's wrong with the world.*

The problem with this is that Jonah doesn't see his own sin, and, most of the time, neither do we. He doesn't see his own ethnic pride and racism because it's flying below his radar. He's part of God's chosen people, he follows the rules, and he's a good guy. He's not whoring around: he's a preacher. If Jonah could see as God sees, he would know that he himself is wearing a black hat just like the Ninevites, and that his only hope is the grace and mercy of God, just like the rest of us. If you could see what God sees, you'd be sporting a black hat too. We're all the bad guys.

What's so shocking in this conservative approach to God, this moralistic way of relating to God through being a good person, is that it is not until everything is taken and our identities blow up that we come to see the reality of our sin. Like I said earlier, as a youth pastor I thought I understood the grace of God. However, it was not until my identity as a successful preacher and leader was removed from me that I realized my life was built upon my own works, my own efforts, and my own pride instead of the grace of God. I was like Jonah, running from the grace of God.

Jonah thought he was a good guy who did good things for God. But this is how you know you are religious and on the run from God: "Everything God tells me to do I'll do…except *this one thing*."

What is your "except that"? Manhattan Pastor Tim Keller often teaches that religious people don't love God for God; they love God for what God can give them.[2] So when God tells us to do the one thing we don't want to do…we run! Jesus tells a story of a rich young ruler to illustrate this. As the rich young ruler comes to Jesus, he asks, "How can I inherit eternal life?"

Jesus tells him some things to do, and the young man says he is already doing all of those things. But Jesus knew the one thing he didn't want to give up, so He told him that to get eternal life he had to give his money to the poor.

How did that encounter end? The rich young ruler went away sad. Why? Because his money meant more to him than grace, which could make him a son of God through Jesus Christ. That is the rich young ruler, and that is Jonah. The rich young ruler loved God to a point, but asking him for his money was a deal breaker.

This is where conservative people often think things like, "I love God, but if He tells me to cross ethnic lines, it's over." Or, "I love God, but if He has a liberal move in right next to me, don't ask me to invite him over for dinner!"

This is where conservatives build up walls that separate people: good/bad, insider/outsider, moral/immoral. And they think that because of their rules they are Christians, but they are not! Christianity is supposed to blow up all of these dividing walls that cause so much hostility in our culture. In fact, God often asks us to do the one thing we don't want to do because He wants to blow up the walls we have built up. But God is gracious! It was gracious of God to help Jonah see that he was living by religion and not grace. It wasn't until God told Jonah to cross racial borders by preaching to the Ninevites that Jonah's cultural and racial elitism was exposed. Jonah thought everything was good, and he didn't even know that he was on the run from God!

One of the first things you discover when you begin to understand the gospel is that these two types of people (and I'm using "liberal" and "conservative" to describe them) are both running from grace. They are both running from God and wanting to be in control of their lives. Control is essentially what it is all about.

Liberals think, "I want to be in control. I want to say what is right for me and what is right for this world. If there is a god, he should do things my way and let me live my life." But conservatives also think, "I want to be in control. If I do good things for God, then I want God to do good things for me."

Both are trying to control God. I hope this is a huge discovery for you. This was the bomb that went off in my life. Moral and religious people have spent the majority of their lives trying to be better than rebels. Conservatives spend so much time trying to be better than the liberals. Liberals spend so much of their time trying to be better than the conservatives. But when the gospel of grace comes in, conservatives begin to hear that all of their do-goodery is just another way to avoid the reality that everyone is a sinner wearing a black hat with no hope except for the grace of God. It shocks them, it humbles them, and it should shake you as well. It should unsettle your life to the core to realize that all your church going, Bible reading, and K-Love music might all actually be attempts to run from God and a relationship with Him that is based completely on grace. For far too long, the church has called the rebellious to repentance and left the self-righteous as they are in their seats. But the God of the Bible calls us all to repentance.

All of us, just like Jonah, must repent of our self-righteousness, our morality, and our do-goodery because they are all just an effort to get God to love us and invite us into His inner circle.

This is the moment in Jonah's life when we will witness an identity implosion. The stealth bomber of sin has been going along unnoticed, and now the bomb is about to be released. This is the day that Jonah's racism will be uncovered; this is the day that he realizes that for his whole life he's felt superior to the Ninevites. All of his good deeds have built up a wall of security around him that makes him feel good about himself. When God asks him to preach to the Ninevites, Jonah runs from God like the "mouse runs from the cat."

> **But Jonah rose to flee to Tarshish from the presence of the LORD. He went down to Joppa and found a ship going to Tarshish. So he paid the fare and went down into it, to go with them to Tarshish, away from the presence of the LORD. (1:3)**

We have seen that we all run from God. The Ninevites (liberal-living) are running in one direction, thinking they are going to find freedom away from the rules and away from the presence of the Lord. Jonah (religious-living) is running in the opposite direction, thinking he is going to find freedom somewhere away from the presence of God.

When the Bible says that Jonah was trying to flee the presence of Yahweh, God, it literally means that he was fleeing from the face of God. This is personal. Jonah is running from a relationship with Yahweh. But God pursues. God's grace is both sovereign and persistent. It isn't convenient. It doesn't always come to us in the ways that we would choose.

For Jonah, the grace of God comes to confront and cross his own will. Let me just tell you this. If you have a god who can't cross your will, you don't know God. You're god. If God can't tell you no, if God can't go against your feelings and go against your thoughts, you don't know God. You are your own god.

For Jonah, the grace of God comes to confront his will and cross him, to stop him in his tracks. He's running in one direction and God's going to chase him down and overtake him. God does this so that Jonah will be loved and receive grace. But in order for that to happen, Jonah has to give up.

Here is where we get to the cure that stops runners in their tracks, gives them rest, and satisfies their souls. *What is it? Is it rules? Religion? Politics?* No, grace captures runners. Grace overtakes sinners. The one-way, undeserved love from God overtakes them. The wholeness and healing and all-satisfying relationship with God that we all desire deep down in our bones don't come delivered up to Jonah the way he wants. God's grace comes to him in a storm.

> **But the LORD hurled a great wind upon the sea, and there was a mighty tempest on the sea, so that the ship threatened to break up. (1:4)**

This is the sovereign God over all of creation. Jonah is trying to run from God, but how do you run from the one who controls the wind and the waves? So God hurls a great wind upon the sea. Whoosh! And there is a mighty tempest, a huge storm that is threatening to break the ship apart. This storm is powerful, but God is showing off just a little bit. Jonah's attempts to flee are about to be crushed, and it looks like everyone on the ship is about to die with him.

> **Then the mariners were afraid, and each cried out to his god. And they hurled the cargo that was in the ship into the sea to lighten it for them. (1:5)**

You have heard the phrase "there are no atheists in foxholes," right? When the waves are coming over the side of the boat, everybody prays. "If you've got a god, you pray to him right now!" We need help; we need saving. First, the sovereign grace of God throws a storm and stops Jonah in his tracks. You might have a storm in your life right now, and God could be trying to stop you in your tracks to get your attention. Second, these pagan, unreligious people are crying out to God while hurling cargo overboard to lighten the ship so that it would float higher in the water.

Where's Jonah?

> **But Jonah had gone down into the inner part of the ship and had lain down and was fast asleep. (1:5)**

The word that is translated as "fast asleep" here actually means "dead asleep." It is the same term that was used when God put Adam to sleep and performed a surgery on him to remove his rib to make Eve. Imagine it as being under anesthesia—lights out. This is more than just a little nap on a boat.

How many of us have been so depressed that all we want to do is sleep? There is a way to sleep that is hiding from reality. You might sleep like this if you have lost something in your life that meant so much to you that all you wanted to do is lie down and die. This is what Jonah is doing. His identity as an Israelite, being a part of God's inner circle, is so important to him that when God hints about including the Ninevites, Jonah becomes despondent. His pride is crushed. He doesn't know who he is anymore, and he is knocked out in the bottom of the boat. Waves are crashing, everyone on the boat is about to die, but the unbelievers are the only ones crying out to God.

> **So the captain came and said to him, "What do you mean, you sleeper? Arise, call out to your god! Perhaps the god will give a thought to us, that we may not perish." (1:6)**

Can you imagine this? The religious man is dead asleep in the bottom of the boat while the rebellious sailors pray for salvation. Furthermore, the captain comes down and rebukes Jonah and commands him to pray! Do you see the sovereignty of God here? God is moving the pieces around on the board. God is in absolute control of the situation.

> **And they said to one another, "Come, let us cast lots, that we may know on whose account this evil has come upon us." (1:7)**

They know this is not a normal storm; the skies were clear and then suddenly were overtaken by an unnatural storm. The sailors themselves know something supernatural is happening.

So, they cast lots and the lot falls on Jonah. Now, I can imagine what Jonah thought in the bottom of the boat, running away from his calling, running away from his identity as a prophet. He probably thought, "Can't I just lie down and die? First, I have this pagan coming in telling me to pray when I don't want to pray. Then they're casting lots and of course it falls to me!"

He can't get away from God! He can't run away from grace! He just can't get away from Him! Then look at this—it just has to be the last straw:

> **So they cast lots, and the lot fell on Jonah. Then they said to him, "Tell us on whose account this evil has come upon us. What is your occupation? And where do you come from? What is your country? And of what people are you?" (1:7-8)**

Those are all identity questions! Who are you? What do you do? As a pastor, those are the questions you don't like to get on an airplane. The guy next to you is dropping "F" bombs, he's on his third Jack and Coke, and he's telling you his story. Then, he inevitably asks, "What do you do?" After I say, "I am a pastor," no more questions the rest of the flight. Nothing. There is an identity that comes with being a pastor. And there's an identity that comes with being God's prophet.

> **And he said to them, "I am a Hebrew, and I fear the LORD, the God of heaven, who made the sea and the dry land." (1:9)**

This is a confession of sorts, more like a catechism answer; obviously he doesn't fear the Lord enough or he wouldn't be on the run. But to some degree he does admit it's his fault. He basically admits, "I am running from God, my identity, and my calling. It is too hard; I don't want to do it. I am too proud, too arrogant, and I don't want to accept the grace of God and believe that I am no better than the Ninevites. So I am on the run!"

> **Then the men were exceedingly afraid and said to him, "What is this that you have done!" For the men knew that he was fleeing from the presence of the LORD, because he had told them. (1:10)**

This is God's confrontational grace. God's grace comes to us in a storm. Jonah wants to go one way, but God loves him too much to leave him to his own folly, so God confronts him. A preacher in the book *Moby Dick* says this: "If we obey God, we must disobey ourselves; and it is in this disobeying ourselves, wherein the hardness of obeying God consists."[3] That is what Jonah is confronted with. He doesn't like the Ninevites, but God says, "Go preach grace to them." He has to disobey his racial pride; he has to disobey his ethnocentricity, and it's hard.

I am going to ask you, has this happened to you yet? Have you been overtaken by the grace of God through the storms in your life in such a way that you've had to disobey yourself? Has God chased you down and overtaken you in the storm?

If you only obey God when it is convenient to you, you haven't been changed by grace. If you only give to the poor when you've got extra money in your pocket, you haven't been changed by grace. If you love only people like yourself, you haven't been changed by grace—or, at least, *haven't been changed enough* by grace.

If God can't ask us to do something that goes against our will and know we will follow through and do it for Him, then we are just like Jonah. We are still trying to use God and live life on our own terms. This is probably the scariest part of this text. You know what God is saying? To receive grace, we must give up control. To receive grace, we have to release the reins of our life over to the sovereign God.

It is interesting to me when I think about it. They're in a boat, the waves are coming, and everyone in the boat is going to die. The only way Jonah dies in this is if he doesn't give up control! If Jonah tries to stay safe and stay in the boat, he dies and everybody with him dies. The whole boat goes under. The only way for Jonah to get the grace, freedom, and salvation that he wants is to confess and stop running.

> **He said to them "Pick me up and hurl me into the sea; then the sea will quiet down for you, for I know it is because of me that this great tempest has come upon you." (1:12)**

Jonah asks these men to pick him up and throw him into the wrath of God, into the storm, into the waters. And surprisingly, it is under the waves that he finds the grace of God waiting for him. See, this story is about Jonah, but it's also about a different man, one who never ran from God. It's about a man who was sinless, but was treated like a sinner. It's about a man who was willing to be thrown overboard into the unrelenting wrath of God in order to save sinners like us. This man is Jesus. Roughly 750 years later Jesus would say in Matthew 12,

> *For as Jonah was three days and three nights in the belly of a huge fish, so the Son of Man will be three days and three nights in the heart of the earth. The men of Nineveh*

> *will stand up at the judgment with this generation and condemn it; for they repented at the preaching of Jonah, and now one greater than Jonah is here. (Matt. 12:40-41)*

What is Jesus saying? Jesus is saying, "I am the true and greater Jonah."

What does that mean? Jonah was thrown into the wrath of God, swallowed up by the sea and a huge fish, and dwelt in the belly of the fish for three days. Jesus Christ was thrown into the wrath of God at the cross, was swallowed up into death, and was in the tomb for three days.

Jonah would be resurrected out of the mouth of a fish and onto safe and dry land.

But Jesus was resurrected out of the grave.

Jesus is the true and better Jonah. Jonah was rescued because Jesus wasn't. Jonah got another chance because Jesus would live the perfect life and die a substitutionary death for him on the cross. Jonah didn't find grace because he cleaned himself up and vowed to live a better life. Jonah found grace because he admitted his sinfulness and allowed himself to be thrown overboard.

And here is the great exchange. For those who admit their sinfulness, have no hope in themselves, but trust only in the grace of God for salvation, they will find Jesus, the true and greater Jonah who was thrown overboard for them. His love is not a metaphor. It's real, and it led Him to the cross where He shows us it's okay to admit our sinfulness. It's okay to say, "I have been running from you and your grace for a long time," because when we look at the cross we see the love of God swallow up our sinfulness and promise a resurrection. The cross shows us that we indeed are so bad that Jesus had to die for us, but we are also so loved that Jesus willingly died for us.

If you are trying to control your life, you are never going to experience this type of love. If you are trying to keep your life as comfortable as possible, you are never going to experience this type of love. Jonah shows us that it's not until we come to the end of ourselves that we find this kind of love, and more times than not this comes in the midst of a storm.

THE FEAR THAT SWALLOWS ALL FEARS

Then the men were exceedingly afraid and said to him, "What is this that you have done!" For the men knew that he was fleeing from the presence of the LORD, because he had told them.

Then they said to him, "What shall we do to you, that the sea may quiet down for us?" For the sea grew more and more tempestuous. He said to them, "Pick me up and hurl me into the sea; then the sea will quiet down for you, for I know it is because of me that this great tempest has come upon you." Nevertheless, the men rowed hard to get back to dry land, but they could not, for the sea grew more and more tempestuous against them. Therefore they called out to the LORD, "O LORD, let us not perish for this man's life, and lay not on us innocent blood, for you, O LORD, have done as it pleased you." So they picked up Jonah and hurled him into the sea, and the sea ceased from its raging. Then the men feared the LORD exceedingly, and they offered a sacrifice to the LORD and made vows.

And the LORD appointed a great fish to swallow up Jonah. And Jonah was in the belly of the fish three days and three nights.

—Jonah 1:10-17

Then the men were exceedingly afraid and said to him, "What is this that you have done!" For the men knew that he was fleeing from the presence of the LORD, because he had told them. (1:10)

If you read through the first chapter of Jonah, you will see the word "fear" or "afraid" several times. It's a dominant theme in the first chapter of the book of Jonah. I think this is something we are all familiar with. It seems to me that there may be no more basic human emotion than fear.

When you read books from a couple hundred years ago, it seems that fear was an everyday concern. Put yourself in their shoes. It was mostly an agrarian society, so there was a lot to be afraid of. You would face a constant fear of bad weather, droughts, floods, tornadoes, and extreme winters that could take your livelihood and life at any time. On top of that, if you wanted to travel far, your travel plans would be wrought with danger. Think of being in a horse and carriage or boat in the ocean—that's freaky! Even a Carnival Cruise liner is a little freaky, and that's a monstrous boat. But imagine being in a rickety old wooden boat for weeks at a time—just crazy! Fear was a constant struggle in their everyday life. Or how about giving birth? It was far more dangerous than it is now with all of the technological advancements that have been made. You might think that we wouldn't deal with fear as much because of modern science and technology, but I don't think we are as free from fear as we might think. Today, with a quick glance at our Facebook feed or *The New York Times*, all of our ancient fears come bubbling up to the surface. They rise up to the surface when we hear about floods, tornadoes, fires, hurricanes, or polar vortexes that threaten our way of life. Then on top of that, we have global issues such as poverty, virus outbreaks, racism, and the Islamic State promoting a violent religious extremism that is set on destroying anyone who doesn't believe like they do.

But let's say you don't pay much attention to those big issues because you're living your life and only looking at things right in front of you. There are always the existential fears, the big questions that are unresolved in our life. Who am I? Why am I here? Who is God? What is He like? Could He actually love someone like me who's done what I've done and been where I've been?

I recently read an interview about actor Shia LaBeouf from the new movie *Fury*. It's an insightful article on many levels. In it, he says that God sovereignly saved him during the filming of *Fury* and has given him a new heart. The article is good, full of cussing, but I enjoyed it anyway. LaBeouf says, "I became a Christian man, and not in a [insert expletives] way—in a very real way. I could have just said the prayers that were on the page. But it was a real thing that really saved me. And you can't identify unless you're really going through it. It's a full-blown exchange of heart, a surrender of control."[4]

Because he played a religious man in the film, he had to read a number of prayers, learn about scripture, and follow a chaplain around. He could have just gone through the motions, but by going through it the way that he did, God sovereignly saved him. I like that because it sounds like something Jesus likes to do.

In another part of the article, LaBeouf explains that he wants to go to college and has even applied three times. When asked why he's never gone, he replies, "Fear."

While he doesn't explicitly state what he is afraid of, he later explains,

> You're only as good as your last thing, and I'm only thinking about the next thing. I've been a runner my whole life, running from myself. Whether to movies or drinking and drugging or...calamity or whatever it is, I've always been running. I'm a dude who loves delusion. It's why I love being an actor—I never have to actually look at myself or be faced with my [problems] or take responsibility.[5]

Now, I would almost say that's insight given only through the Holy Spirit. LaBeouf can see into his own heart in such a way as to say, "I'm running from my issues. I'm afraid of real life and being in these movies is a form of delusion for me, it's a way to deliver me from this fear of failure, from this fear of being normal, this fear of being forgotten." LaBeouf 's wealthy; he's popular; he's successful; but it seems that he's so afraid of people forgetting him and of being a failure in his own eyes that he can't even take a break to do something he really wants to do. He's trapped by his fear, and up until his last movie his acting was his savior. His acting was his way to save himself from his fear of failure. Acting was his self-salvation project, his religion. It was his way to deal with his fears on his own.

What we're going to find out in our study of Jonah is that, whether we are non-religious or religious, there are only two ways to deal with our fears: 1) through religion (working them out on our own), or 2) through God drowning our fears in the power of the gospel. Those are the only two ways. Religion is about me and my effort while the gospel is all about Jesus and His effort for us on the cross.

I read the following scripture recently, and it lodged itself in my heart. Proverbs 29:25 says, "The fear of man is a snare." Now, a snare is a little trap for different animals; let's just say a rabbit. As the rabbit is running along on their little rabbit trail, the way they've always run, they get caught up in the snare, and they're immobilized. Typically, they strangle and die. Proverbs says that the fear of man is like that. When our fears grip us, they immobilize us—they keep us from moving forward into things that God wants for us, and they can even kill us. Today, we're going to learn how to let God drown our fears. They are too great for us to deal with, but He can drown them.

In the beginning of the book of Jonah, we learned that Jonah was a prophet of God, but he was on the run. He was a religious guy who, on the outside, looked sharp; he looked like a good guy. He was a moral and God-fearing person, but deep down in Jonah's bones, he lived with an ethnic and racial superiority that caused him to actually run from God. He was religious.

Keller says religion is basically saying to God that we will do something for Him and then He has to bless us.[6] Religious people think, "God, You must give me a good life, You need to do things my way. I'll pray, give, go to church, and be moral, but I expect You to bless my life. You have to clear the rocks out of my path, make it straight, and give me success in whatever I want."

Religion is a self-salvation project. It's a way for us to save ourselves from fear. Jonah's greatest fear is this city that's outside of Israel: Nineveh, the capital of Assyria. Remember, Nineveh was Israel's sworn enemy and a huge threat to its peace and prosperity. Jonah did not want these people being forgiven by God and brought into God's family. He hated the Assyrians. They were the Islamic State of his day. When God told him to go preach to Israel's sworn enemy, Jonah flipped. That's the one thing he wouldn't do for God. So, Jonah runs from God in the opposite direction to Tarshish.

Here, in this story, we really get a glimpse of the great problem with religion. Religion—I'm going to say it a bunch—is a self-salvation project. It's a way for me to save myself from my fears. So, Jonah desperately needs and wants and craves to be an insider with God (and to be an insider, there have to be outsiders, right?). For Jonah, all of his morality and all of his religious service were just his ways to save himself from his fear of being on the outside. He thought, "I'm accepted by God because I'm a good person." So when God tells him to go preach to these bad people and bring these bad people in, it just short circuits him. He can't handle it.

See, religious, moralistic people follow God for what God can give them. They don't love God for God; they use God to get what they really love. For Jonah, his love was his feeling of moral and ethnic superiority. He wanted to be an insider with God, so he was willing to use God to feel like an insider, to feel good enough and accepted. He didn't love God for God.

But God is so gracious, and so loving, and so kind that he doesn't let us be satisfied with religion. He loves Jonah too much to let him live out his life with this religious mindset, so he pushes on the very thing Jonah doesn't want him to push on. God goes after his racial and ethnic superiority. He's got to teach this brother the difference between grace and religion. God is pressing on it because He wants to take that racism and drown it. He wants to take that fear and drown it.

Like most religious folk (any of us that struggle to be religious), Jonah is stubborn, he is proud, and he is hard-hearted. Jonah shows us that you can look like a really good person on the outside but still run from God in your heart. You can be consistently attending church, you can be really moral, but you can still be on the run from God in your heart. What really matters to God is what's going on in your heart.

Jonah (and any religious person, by extension) responds in

three ways when God addresses his fear: 1) run, 2) sleep, and 3) die.

First, Jonah tries to run from his problems. If you believe that you have been really, really good, and then you either fall into some kind of sin or God does something in your life that you are not happy with, one of the first things you do is run from God. You run from God because you are angry at Him.

Second, Jonah tries to sleep his problems away. If you've ever tried sleep therapy, you know how this works. This is when you pull the covers over your head and try to sleep until noon, hoping that a little more sleep will make things better. We feel ashamed or depressed, so we try to sleep it off in despair.

Third, Jonah tries to escape his problems by death. By the end of the chapter, Jonah's like, "Okay, it's me. Throw me in. Just kill me." He literally tells them to throw him in the water. It's funny because this isn't Jonah being super heroic and gracious. He would rather die than have Nineveh be saved. See, that's what happens when our self-salvation projects fail us, when our marriage that we thought was going to be perfect fails us. We often run from God; we try to sleep it off; and sometimes we get so low, we want to end it all. We want to be gone. We want it to be over. That's what happens when self-salvation projects fail us. And so we see Jonah, the religious man, get rebellious. He can't get his way, so he runs from God. To further complicate things, we see the rebellious get religious.

Now I want to look at the anti-heroes in this story, the sailors. What's your opinion of a sailor? The one thing I have heard about sailors is that saying, "He cusses like a sailor." That usually doesn't mean that they use "Christian cuss words" either. In fact, it usually means that person drops the "F" bomb a lot. I just flipped on the television the other night and there was a show on the Discovery channel with sailors in it and just about every other word was getting bleeped out. For whatever reason, sailors know how to cuss. When we're looking at these sailors or these mariners, that's the type of people we're looking at. We're looking at the anti-hero, the antithesis to Jonah. The sailors are everything Jonah's not: Jonah was moral; the sailors are immoral. Jonah was religious; the sailors are rebellious. Jonah knew God, at least intellectually, but these sailors don't know God at all. Jonah was the insider; the sailors are the outsiders.

Furthermore, what's really interesting in this story is that by the time we get to verse 5, the religious man rebels, and the rebels get religious. The first thing these rebellious sailors do when they think they're going to drown is cry out to their gods—that's plural. They were polytheistic in their beliefs. They believed in a god of the sea, a god of the sun, and a god of the clouds. They had probably even brought their own little idols onboard.

These are the type of people that don't go to church and don't want organized religion, but the first thing that happens when they encounter a life-threatening storm is that they get religious and cry out to their gods. For us the storm could be something like divorce, or the loss of a child, or the loss of a job, or the threat of Ebola, or Islamic State. For the sailors, it was an epic storm. So what did they do? They got religious. See, this is what Romans 1 teaches us. Everyone, every human being, is religious deep down. Even rebellious people. When they get afraid, their response, their trigger response, their gut reaction, is to get religious.

Human beings have been built *imago dei*, in the image of God. We've been hardwired by God to believe in Him. We don't instinctively know what He's like. But we do have this vague notion that He's powerful, He's up there, He's the creator, and we owe Him something. But we need to be taught the gospel and the word of God to know what God is actually like.

So the storm hits, and the sailors get real religious. I'm reminded of that cartoon about Christ coming back for His church where the characters are heard saying, "Oh, Jesus is coming! Look busy!" That's kind of what's going on here. Even the captain is running through the ship making sure everyone is praying to their gods.

We do the same thing when adversity strikes. Our marriage hits a rough patch; our kids start going down the wrong direction; we lose a job; a family member gets cancer; so we pray—we get religious! No matter how rebellious you are, your gut reaction is to get religious—but religion isn't enough. Praying in some general way isn't enough to take away your fears. Because we are all born in sin, we have a dulled image of God, a corrupt concept of who God is. We think that God only loves good people and wants to destroy bad people. If you do happen to be good enough, somehow, you cross an imaginary line into an "inner circle." Most of us spend the majority of our lives thinking that the line for being good enough is somewhere just behind our heels. Anybody who's a little worse than me is going to hell and anybody who's the slightest bit better than me, well, I'm on my way to becoming more like them. Deep down we all think that what God really wants from us is to be good, moral, hardworking people. If you want to be on God's good side, you better get your act together.

Now, listen. That is a fear-based concept of how to relate to God. Religion is a fear-based way of relating to God that makes God into our self-salvation project—He becomes the way for us to manage our fears. It's like this: if you have been a high achiever all of your life who has been primarily motivated by a deep-seated fear of failure, you can try to turn God into your self-salvation strategy. You go to Him in hopes that He will keep failure far from you. You might even cut out all the scriptures that talk about success and blessing and paste them on your mirror. This is evidence you aren't going to God for God, but you are going to Him because you don't want to fail.

Listen to how Keller describes this: "The essence of fear-based religion is to say, 'God, I will do anything you want if only you'll help me in this way.' Help me get married, help me with my children, keep me safe, help me in my career. I'll do [blank] if you do [blank]." Keller goes on, "What is so ironic and paradoxical about saying, 'I'll do anything if,' is the very statement proves you won't do the one thing God wants. 'What do you mean?' The one thing God wants is you to love him without 'ifs.' When you say, 'I'll do anything if…' the one thing you won't do is to love him without ifs.'"[7]

You will never be free from fear unless you love Him without "ifs," because when you say, "God, I'll do this and I'll do anything if," do you know what's on the other side of the "if"? Your real god.

When you say, "I'll do anything if you keep my marriage together," your real god is your marriage. Or, "I'll do anything if I'm successful in this career," your real god is your career. Or, "I'll do anything if you make me financially prosperous," your real god is your money.

Do you see that? That's where these sailors are at when we meet them. They don't know or love God for God—they just don't want to die and will call on any god necessary to save them from their fear. This is going to show us why religion doesn't work. Religion doesn't deliver us from our fears—it multiplies them.

After the sailors get religious and start praying, they find Jonah in the bottom of the boat and begin to ask him all kinds of questions to find out if he's the reason they are in this mess. Jonah admits that he is God's prophet and on the run from Him, and verse 10 says, "Then the men were exceedingly afraid." Their brief foray into religion has actually multiplied their fears. Now they are "exceedingly afraid" because they are harboring a fugitive on the run from "the LORD, the God of heaven, who made the sea and the dry land." If we have a religious view of God where He punishes bad people and gives grace to good people but then realize we are the bad people, our fears will be multiplied! The sailors must have thought, "I have failed God, and now I am going to pay for it with my life." Religious people and religion make people only more neurotic. They don't actually take care of your fear.

Now here you might be saying, "That's exactly why I'm not religious. Religion is all fear-based! That's why I don't go to church, unless I get drug there by my girlfriend or my boyfriend or to appease my parents." Well, these sailors aren't church-goers either. The sailors aren't religious types either, but look how religion is deeply embedded in their hearts. They can't get away from it. When the storms of life come, when danger arises, when their fear erupts, their religion surfaces. It's like they can't even help it. Religion is anything I use to save myself from my deepest fears. It could be building bunkers and stockpiling pork and beans.

Have you seen the shows on television about people who are prepared for WWIII? They are preparing for an IS invasion, or a solar flare, or a stock market crash that will send us back to a great depression. They say, "We need to be prepared. We need to carry machine guns and we need to stockpile two years' worth of bottled water." Do we really? Maybe. But does that deliver you from your fears? I am here to tell you, the people on these shows do not look less afraid; in fact, they scare me! They don't look very neighborly—you could knock on their door to borrow sugar and end up getting shot. Their preparation is their religion. It's made everybody outside of their camp a possible threat. Our human ways to deal with fear only multiply our fear. Self-salvation projects never work. I wish we could believe that.

Shia LaBeouf believed one more movie was his answer. That one more movie, one more starring role was going to make him feel like a man and give him what he longed for, but it never worked. It couldn't take away his fear. That was his self-salvation project. Religion never works. It's the same for us; our attempts to deliver ourselves from our fears never work. However, there is something that can drown our fears, and it's totally different from religion. But before I tell you what it is, I want to pause here a minute to think about something.

Do you think or have you ever thought that religion and Christianity were the same thing? They are not. Every other world religion, every other way you save yourself, is religious. Christianity is something totally different. It has its own category. No other world religion, no other way to save yourself has what Christianity has at the center: Jesus Christ, yes, but it's also what He brings—grace.

> **Then they said to him, "What shall we do to you, that the sea may quiet down for us?" For the sea grew more and more tempestuous. He said to them, "Pick me up and hurl me into the sea; then the sea will quiet down for you, for I know it is because of me that this great tempest has come upon you." (1:11-12)**

These sailors are freaking out! They were scared enough already before hearing about Jonah's God. Now they're even more scared. But Jonah tells them to hurl him into the sea, and then the sea will quiet down for them.

Now, most scholars say that Jonah is not being gracious here. Jonah does not want to fulfill the mission of God. He would rather them throw him in the sea and die than preach to the Ninevites. But look how these sailors respond.

> **Nevertheless, the men rowed hard to get back to dry land, but they could not, for the sea grew more and more tempestuous against them. (1:13)**

The sailors were given the way of salvation, but they turned from Jonah, gripped their oars, and rowed harder. How many times do people come into a church and hear a preacher say, "Nothing can save you but the grace of Jesus. Nothing can save you but the mercy of God. You cannot save yourself; you must believe by faith in Jesus Christ, receive the righteousness of God by faith, and stand only in the righteousness of Jesus. That's how you relate to God." We hear that message, but then turn from it to our own moral efforts. We believe that if we try harder, and live better, or go to church more often, we can save ourselves.

We need to hear this truth: there is no peace or comfort in religion. There is no rest in trying harder and rowing faster. This is the automatic response of people's hearts. They hear the gospel and respond religiously. There are only two types of people in the world. There are religious people, and there are Christians. You might think, "Oh, there are non-religious people." No, no, no. Everybody is religious. They're using something to save themselves from their fears.

But God in His grace sends tempestuous storms to His people to obliterate their self-salvation projects. He puts them on an open sea where there's no hope, they are going to drown, and their greatest fear is going to be realized; that is, unless they believe in the one who was thrown into the storm for them.

Jesus, the Father, and the Holy Spirit are trying to teach us the difference between religion and grace. Religion is always trying harder so that God will bless you. But then when things go bad for you, you're powerless. The only answer is to give up like Jonah, sleep in the bottom of the boat, and wish for death, or try harder like the sailors. "I'll do better next time. I'll try harder. I'll learn from my mistakes." But grace drowns our fears in the love of God. Now, how does that look?

Look again at the verse. They're rowing hard trying to "get back to dry land, but they could not, for the sea grew more and more tempestuous against them." God is against their moral self-effort to save themselves. God is opposed to their saving themselves. They're not going to do it. They're going to drown. It's imminent. What do they do? They call out to the Lord.

> **Therefore they called out to the LORD, "O LORD, let us not perish for this man's life, and lay not on us innocent blood, for you, O LORD, have done as it pleased you." So they picked up Jonah and hurled him into the sea, and the sea ceased from its raging. (1:14-15)**

Remember, before this they had prayed to their gods, little 'g' and plural. Now, they called out to Yahweh, Jonah's God, the uncreated creator. They called out to the one God, then picked up Jonah and hurled him into the sea.

If you've ever watched *Deadliest Catch*, you know what this might look like. They are on the deck, the storm is up, and the boat is rocking. And today's boats are way more reliable than what Jonah and the sailors had. It is super dangerous today when squalls come up and there's ice everywhere. How much more chaotic would it have been for people back then? Those sailors just knew they were going to die. All their self-salvation projects failed them. All their other gods failed them. Their one last hope is faith and repentance in this God, Yahweh. So, they take this bloke and throw him overboard. As soon as

Jonah hits the water, boom! The sea becomes still. The wind suddenly stops. How do these professional fishermen and sailors respond?

> **Then the men feared the LORD exceedingly, and they offered a sacrifice to the LORD and made vows. (1:16)**

This is not what you would expect. What you expect is this: fear, more fear, more fear, deliverance from fear. Peace. But what happens is: fear, more fear, more fear, and fearing God exceedingly. What just happened? This is the fear that swallows all other fears. This is the fear that drowns all other fears. Fearing God and being afraid of God are totally different. This is awe. This is worship. See, when people are saved by grace, worship happens. Then, they offer sacrifices to God. That's when you know you've been impacted by grace. Worship happens.

The only other option is the self-salvation project, and worship doesn't happen that way. You always feel obligated to do more and you're never quite good enough. The psalmist talks about a healthy fear of God as well by saying, "But with you there is forgiveness that you may be feared" (Ps. 130:4). This is the fear that captures our imagination and hearts and causes us to respond in worship. Rowing hard to save yourself never leads you to worship.

Now, how does this text show us how to be delivered from our fears? These sailors show us it's not through religion; it's not through our own effort. It's through a personal experience of being saved from your greatest fear at the complete and total expense of someone else. That's how you defeat your fears. Someone else drowns for you.

This is how Christianity is different from religion. This is the gospel according to Jonah. Jesus Christ is the true and better Jonah. Jesus was willingly thrown into the wrath of God for us to save us. Jesus proves to us that God actually loves us and God has provided a way for us to love Him.

You may not even realize it, but at the bottom of your soul your greatest fear is that God cannot love you. I've been telling my friends a lot lately that God is totally into them. It just makes people squirm. As Christians, God is pleased with us because of the work of His Son. He's happy; there's a smile on His face. He wants to know you and He wants you to know Him. He wants to love you and He wants you to love Him. He doesn't want your white-knuckled obedience. I think all of us have to see Jesus in the place of Jonah and us as the sailors. We're trying to save ourselves, but we see Jesus thrown overboard for us. We have to be captured by that.

But how? How do you do this? What's your greatest fear? Are you afraid of failure, of not being accepted? That your child will die? That your spouse will leave you first? Are you afraid of being broke? The answer to your fears is to see Jesus thrown into them for you. Jesus has been thrown into our worst fears already! He's experienced loneliness, separation, ridicule, humiliation, and poverty. He was whipped, stabbed, and crucified on a cross for us. Whatever our fears are, Jesus has felt them and carried them through the cross to eternity. He died with them, and He rose up out of them promising to weather life's storms with us.

No matter what your fear is, the only way out is to see Jesus thrown into it for you. We need to meditate on that: Jesus went through it all. He loved you so much that He died for you. We don't have to fear shame or ridicule, because we stand in the righteousness of God. God loves us no matter what happens in our lives. We have the strong foundation that we are loved and accepted through the perfect work of Jesus on our behalf.

So, why is it that many of us reject Jesus and want to save ourselves? Why is it that, when the sailors heard Jonah was the solution to their problem, they chose to row? It is because we will do anything in our power not to need God's grace. If our total salvation is a result of what Jesus has done for us, then how could we refuse anything He would ask of us?

Shia LaBeouf said it right. When I receive grace I'm giving up control of my life. This means that God can say, "Go to Nineveh." He can say, "Stay right there in that marriage and work it out." He can say, "Stay in that job," or, "Stay in that church." He could tell me to do anything. How can I refuse Him if it's all grace? That's what we're afraid of—losing control. We would rather save ourselves, but self-salvation projects always fail. Nothing smaller than God can give us the freedom and the fulfillment that we're looking for.

Let me finish that verse I mentioned earlier, Proverbs 29:25. It says this: "The fear of man lays a snare, but whoever trusts in the LORD is safe." Jesus can save you if you put your faith in Him. This is a daily faith, not a one-time, get your Jesus card and walk out kind of faith. This is an every day putting your faith in Him as He puts your fears to death through the power of the gospel.

If you've been trying to save yourself from your own fears, I encourage you to remove your trust from that self-salvation project, and put your trust in Jesus—surrender your way. This is the craziness of Christianity. There is no ladder to climb to be a Christian. It's repentance and belief. It's grace. It's been done for you already in Christ. Put your faith in Him. The Apostle John saw this and said, "There is no fear in love, but perfect love casts out all fear" (I John 4:18). The only true salvation, the only true freedom from our fears, can be found by being rescued by Jesus.

FOUR MARKS OF REAL PRAYER

And the LORD appointed a great fish to swallow up Jonah. And Jonah was in the belly of the fish three days and three nights. Then Jonah prayed to the LORD, his God, from the belly of the fish saying, "I called out to the LORD out of my distress and He answered me. Out of the belly of Sheol I cried and you heard my voice. Where you cast me into the deep, into the heart of the seas, and the flood surrounded me; all your waves and your billows passed over me. Then I said, 'I am driven away from your sight; yet I shall again look upon your holy temple.' The waters closed in over me to take my life. The deep surrounded me. Weeds were wrapped around my head at the roots of the mountains. I went down to the land whose bars closed upon me forever. Yet you brought my life up from the pit, oh LORD, my God. When my life was feigning away, I remembered the LORD and my prayer came to you, into your holy temple. Those who pay regard to vain idols forsake their hope of steadfast love. But I with the voice of thanksgiving will sacrifice to you; what I have vowed I will pay. Salvation belongs to the LORD!"

And the LORD spoke to the fish and it vomited Jonah out upon the dry land. Then the word of the LORD came to Jonah the second time saying, "Arise, go to Nineveh, that great city, and call out against it the message that I tell you." So Jonah arose and went to Nineveh, according to the word of the LORD.

—Jonah 1:17-3:3

Jonah is an interesting book, isn't it? We've got the preacher, we've got the prophet, the goody two-shoes, the moral, upright, conservative, buttoned-up, and laced-tight man running from God. He runs from grace, but Jonah obviously must have forgotten Theology 101. How do you run from the face of a God who's omnipresent? That is a problem. Jonah runs *from* God, but in actuality, because God is great and sovereign, Jonah actually runs right *into* God. You can't outrun omnipresence! He's everywhere all at the same time! Many of us grew up with the idea that God was "after me." I had this idea of God when I grew up. I was scared of Him and imagined He was just waiting to zap me or break my leg or something.

When Jonah runs, God pursues him, but He doesn't do it to punish Jonah. He is not chasing Jonah down to ruin his life. God is instead trying to free Jonah from the most constricting thing in the entire world: religion. God is trying to heal Jonah from his own self-righteousness and his feelings of superiority over people of other nationalities. God is trying to take their relationship to the next level. He's chasing him down to teach the one lesson that must be learned and relearned, experienced and re-experienced: *that grace is what our hearts are longing for and grace can only be found through weakness and humility.* That is the only place you can find grace. In fact, this text shows us most of the time that grace is found in the dark.

God calls Jonah to preach grace, but before he can preach it, he has to receive it. He has to be a grace-shaped man. He needs to feel down deep in his bones that God loves sinners. Unless Jonah experiences the grace of God, he will never be able to communicate that grace to the Ninevites. So God does what He normally does when people don't understand grace…He sends a giant fish to swallow Jonah. Wait, what?

> **And the LORD appointed a great fish to swallow up Jonah. And Jonah was in the belly of the fish three days and three nights. (1:17)**

"The LORD appointed." God directed a fish to swallow His boy, Jonah, who had just been thrown over the side of the boat. Jonah was in the belly of the fish three days and three nights. Can this even happen? Is this just a myth, a fairy tale, or something in the Bible that is just ridiculous?

Now if you already believe in God, and you believe the God of the Bible, then you know all things are possible. God can do whatever God wants to do. But, if you are reading this book as a non-believer, this is a very hard story to believe, isn't it? A fish swallows a man. He's in the belly of the fish for three days and then suddenly he is spit back up.

If you happen to own a set of the *Encyclopedia Britannica*, or the free encyclopedia known as "Google," you can see examples of this very thing happening. It's very interesting. In your research, you'll find that an average sperm whale has a mouth that is 20 feet long, 15 feet high, and 9 feet wide. That is bigger than many of our bedrooms!

Ambrose John Wilson also relates the following fascinating story. In 1891 a ship called Star of the East spotted a large sperm whale by the Falkland Islands. They dispatched two boats to go and harpoon this whale. During their effort, one of these boats capsized, a sailor drowned, and another man, James Bartley, disappeared. They had no idea what happened to him. The sailors on the other boat harpooned the whale, dragged it aboard the main vessel, and were cutting up the whale to remove the blubber. The next day they cut into the belly of the whale, and when it opened, out came James Bartley, unconscious but alive! They used seawater to revive him, and he went back to work in a couple of days. He was in the belly of that whale overnight. Was that comfortable? I doubt it. He wasn't throwing a party in there. It was very difficult. But after thoroughly researching the story of James Bartley and the likelihood of a man living through such an ordeal, Wilson concludes, "It is perfectly possible for a man to be swallowed alive and after an interval vomited up again, also for him to remain alive for two or three days within the whale."[8]

I could discuss other examples, but I don't want us to miss the main point that the book of Jonah is not about a whale or a fish. In fact, in this four-chapter story, only three verses even mention the whale: 1:17, 2:1, and 2:10. This story is actually about the internal struggle of a religious man, Jonah.

Jonah's relationship with God has been based on something other than grace, and now his entire life has blown up. He's (to use a term that Christians like to use) backslidden. He's mad at God and on the run, but God is no chump. God is no pushover. God's will is always effective; that's what it means to be sovereign. We can fight against it, we can push back against it, we can run from it, and even resist it in some ways, but God's grace overcomes our resistance. God knows how to back us into a corner and get us, each and every one of us, in situations and circumstances that cause us to reevaluate our lives so we will experience grace.

That is where our guy Jonah is: in the belly of a hot, smelly fish rethinking everything. Scientists say it would be about 108 degrees in there and cramped. The digestive fluids would be irritating his skin. It would be pitch black with water sloshing around. I imagine he is pretty overwhelmed in his situation, poised for listening, wouldn't you agree? It's here in the dark that Jonah once again finds grace.

> **Then Jonah prayed to the LORD his God, from the belly of the fish.** (2:1)

From Jonah's life, we can learn two ways to pray: there's a religious way and then there's what Jonah is about to do. It's hard to see the difference. Jonah has been a religious person, he's been obeying God and following the rules and now, all of a sudden, Jonah wakes up in his own personal hell. Have you ever experienced this? Have you ever woken up one day, and you've been obeying the rules, you've been going along life as normal, but then one morning everything is not right? That's what's going on with Jonah. Three days and three nights in the belly of a fish and he finally gets real.

Have you ever had a moment like this? Have you ever woken up from a drunken night out in someone else's bed or woken up to your business dangling on the edge of bankruptcy? Have you woken up to your spouse handing you divorce papers? And you are surprised because you don't even know how you got there. You might even think, "I wasn't raised like this. I know better. Where did I get so off track? What has happened to me?" I can imagine this buttoned-up preacher man waking up in the belly of a whale thinking the same things.

Remember, religion is this: "I'll do/only if." It's pretty easy to see the difference between that and Christianity on paper. Christianity has nothing to do with what you do because Christianity has been done for you. Jesus Christ died your death that you deserved for your rebellion against Him. Jesus Christ took your place, and upon the cross He took all the punishment on Himself and died in your place so that you could receive the steadfast love of the Lord.

The problem, however, is we can be living by religion and not even realize it. Thankfully, it's at this time that God sends storms into our lives. He takes the lights out. He makes things go dark so that we're forced to address our self-righteousness. We're forced to look and search and find grace in the dark. That's exactly what's going on with Jonah.

You might be in a dark spot. You might be in a really difficult season of your life. You might be in the belly of a whale so to speak; things feel like your own personal hell. If you are, I want you to know that there is grace there. God's presence is there. If you're not there now, you will be. You will be going along in life all buttoned-up and feeling good about yourself just like Jonah was.

Suffering comes for us all. It's either in your past, your present, or it is in your future. We are all going to suffer. We are all going to be in a dark spot where nothing will help us but the grace of God. And that's where we find Jesus. That's where our hearts are formed and shaped and we get an identity that can't be moved.

In the hand of God, suffering *can* have a redemptive purpose in our life. I'm not saying suffering is good. I'm not glorifying suffering. I'm saying suffering can have a redemptive good. I've met people that have had cancer, and you've probably heard them say something to the effect of, "Cancer was the best thing that ever happened to me." Suffering can be used by God as smelling salts to wake us up because there's nothing like suffering to make us feel helpless. Now, why would I want to feel helpless? According to Richard Foster, "Helplessness is the real secret and the impelling power of prayer."[9] O. Hallesby in his famous book on prayer says this: "Prayer and helplessness are inseparable. Only those who are helpless can truly pray."[10]

Most Americans, most of the time, do not feel helpless. There is always a way out. If you are in bankruptcy, just talk to the right lawyer; there are tricks to getting out of difficult situations. We don't really feel helpless most of the time.

However, Jonah is in the belly of a whale. Can you imagine? Only Jack Bauer could find his way out of this situation. He is in the belly of a whale, there is no hope, and his ears are popping as the whale descends deeper and deeper. There is no way out; he feels absolutely helpless.

What Jonah found in this situation, and what we need, is *real prayer*. Jesus talks about how children do this kind of prayer in Matthew 18. Have you ever been around children when they pray? They are so honest when they pray sometimes it is hilarious. It's often the funniest time of my night. An honest prayer from a child might be, "God, Suzie made fun of me at school, would you make her ugly tonight?" That's a legitimate prayer from a child. But I think that kind of prayer is more acceptable to God than when I feel hatred for someone but pray, "God, would you please change her heart so she will never do things like that to me again?" In prayer, we will say "the right thing" while children will say the true thing.

Paul Miller in *A Praying Life* says that "Private, personal prayer is one of the last great bastions of religion, of legalism. In order to pray like a child, you might need to unlearn the non-personal, non-real praying that you've been taught."[11] That's what we are aiming at through Jonah. I want us to unlearn the non-real praying.

Jonah shows us how to really pray. His prayer has at least four key parts that are crucial to experiencing the grace of God when you're in a dark place. Jonah 1) assesses where he is, 2) confesses what got him there, 3) remembers the gospel, and 4) responds in worship.

First, Jonah honestly assesses where he is. In the past, theologians called this meditation. Not mystic or eastern meditation, which is emptying your mind. This is taking scripture that you have either memorized or are reading and pressing it down into your heart. Thinking about it, stirring it over, wrestling with it, and praying from that place. Almost all of Jonah's prayers are from the psalms. He's been taught the psalms as a child, he's been singing them throughout his lifetime, and they have shaped his prayer life. The psalms are songs that were written down and are sung to this day as honest prayers. Jonah takes this scripture from memory, wrestles with it, digests it, and then releases his prayer.

> **I called out to the LORD, out of my distress, and he answered me; out of the belly of Sheol I cried, and you heard my voice. (2:2)**

Sheol is the place of the dead. It represents hell. Jonah is saying that he is in his own personal hell right now. This is honesty.

> **For you cast me into the deep, into the heart of the seas, and the flood surrounded me; all your waves and your billows passed over me. (2:3)**

Perhaps you didn't catch it, but Jonah 1 was all about man's perspective. Who threw Jonah into the sea? The sailors, right? But in chapter 2, we will see things from God's sovereign perspective. Jonah acknowledges that even though those men threw him in the sea, God was the one who did it.

> **Then I said, "I am driven away from your sight; yet I shall again look upon your holy temple." (2:4)**

Isn't that interesting? Jonah was trying to flee from the face of the LORD in chapter 1, but now that Jonah is finally getting the distance he wants he starts to realize that it is not what he wanted after all! It's like the smelling salts of suffering wake him up and he finds he is in a dark spot and only going deeper. The hell surrounding him is crushing him, and he feels like he is on the brink of death. He is now, for the first time, clearly assessing his situation and realizing he is in a dark place because he has been running from God.

> **The waters closed in over me to take my life; the deep surrounded me; weeds were wrapped about my head at the roots of the mountains. I went down to the land whose bars closed upon me forever. (2:5)**

Jonah finally realizes that he is in absolute hell without God's grace and mercy. Have you ever felt like that? Thank God that the Bible gives us language to honestly express what is really going on in us and around us without being fake. This is step one of real prayer: we assess where we are with God.

Second, we confess what got us there. At Sacred City Church we say it like this, "You've got to own your sin." What does that mean?

> **Those who pay regard to vain idols forsake their hope of steadfast love. (2:8)**

Owning your sin means admitting you are a bad guy. When Jonah experienced this he finally realized he had been worshiping something other than God. He was just like the Ninevites!

This is the moment in real prayer when you realize all the stuff that's going on outside of you is not always what is victimizing you. You are not always an innocent victim. If you could see things from God's perspective, you would see that sometimes things are the way they are due to your own making. For prayer to be real, we must see ourselves not only as sufferers, but also as sinners. What I mean is that we must confess both our sinful actions and our sinful heart motivations. This has been called the "sin below the sin." It's the *why* behind what you did.

Any time something becomes more important to you than your relationship with God, it becomes an idol. Idols aren't just little statues that people in third world countries use. An idol is anything in your life that means more to you than God. Idols can even be good things that we begin to love too much that become bad things in our life.

For Jonah, running from God was just the fruit from the tree of his life. The problem was actually down at the root of his belief in God. If you have bad apples on your tree, you can't just pull the fruit off, go to Walmart, and buy new apples to replace the bad ones. You have to get to the root of the problem. Idolatry is the root of the issue. This means you can't just go after the fruit.

You can't just confess the fruit. You can't just say you're sorry for yelling at your wife, or not teaching your kids the scriptures, or cheating on your taxes. For it to be real prayer, you have to confess the heart of idolatry underneath the behavior. You have to see that the reason you're cheating on your taxes is because you are an idolater who has been worshiping money. That's why a person cheats on their taxes. That's why someone robs God by not giving him tithes and offerings. If you don't go through this step and get to the sin beneath the sin, you're not actually praying. You're just being religious. Religious people do bad things, feel ashamed, make resolutions to never do them again, and then try harder. But they still do them. That's a man-centered attempt to get God on your side. It's not grace; it's not the gospel. Christians assess where they are in light of

God's word and then confess the sins beneath their sins. "In that moment I was worshiping something other than You, God. The approval of man meant more to me in that moment than Your approval of me." This is why Jonah says he forsook his hope of steadfast love.

There's no other God than the One True God, and for Him we use a big "G," but for every other thing worshiped that is not God we use a little "g." No other god gives grace. If you worship money and you fail it, it will be gone. It will crush you; it will empty you; it will take everything from you and leave you penniless. It's not personal; it's just business. There's no grace. If you worship your children, when you fail them—and you will—one day they're going to turn against you. They are going to point to you when things don't go well for them and blame you. They will hate you or believe with all their heart that you hate them. It is going to crush you. There's no grace with little "g" gods.

But Jonah shows us that with God it is different. This is unbelievable. When we fail and run from God, He doesn't leave us. When we fail, He actually comes after us. He orchestrates the whole universe to get us connected back to His grace through real prayer. This is how persistent, powerful, sovereign, and gracious God is. Nothing else that we can serve will give us this grace.

Third, remember the gospel. This whole chapter in Jonah is littered with hope.

> **I called out to the LORD, out of my distress, and he answered me. (2:1)**

Jonah's in his own personal hell, cries out to God, and God answers him. In the storm, in the darkness, God responds, and Jonah can hear it in his heart.

> **Out of the belly of Sheol I cried, and you heard my voice. For you cast me into the deep, into the heart of the seas, and the flood surrounded me; all your waves and your billows passed over me. Then I said, "I am driven away from your sight; yet I shall again look upon your holy temple." (2:2b-4)**

If you were wondering what this temple business is about, let me help you. The temple is the place where men met with God. Inside the temple, men and women would have their sins forgiven. But the way their sins were forgiven was through an animal taking their punishment by having its neck cut and shedding its blood. When Jonah realizes his sin, he confesses, "This is what I deserve, to be swallowed up and killed inside of this whale, to go to the bottom of the deep, into hell itself because I rebelled against God." But it is also in this moment that he remembers the temple, the place where God forgives sin. He remembers God's grace-filled nature. He remembers the gospel of Old Testament times: his sacrifice, his substitute on the altar in the temple.

> **I went down to the land whose bars closed upon me forever; yet you brought up my life from the pit, O LORD, my God.** (2:6) **Salvation belongs to the LORD!** (2:9)

Finally, after realizing the depths of his own sin, Jonah acknowledges that salvation belongs to God. Jonah's mind drifts back to the temple and remembers the work that God has done to save him.

There is quite a big difference between us and Jonah, though. We have the benefit of knowing that 750 years after this, God sent his Son, Jesus Christ, to be the ultimate sacrifice on the altar for us. Jonah looked to the temple, but we look to Jesus. Jesus is the temple where mankind can meet with God. But Jesus is also more than the temple. He is our sacrifice on the altar, He is our substitute, He is the one who takes our place and turns away the wrath of God that we deserve for our rebellion and idol worship. We deserve to drown for our sins, but Jesus drowned in the wrath of God for us.

It's in the moment of realizing this that our prayer turns from religious to gospel-centered, from non-real to real. There are only two places our punishment can go: 1) on Jesus, or 2) on us. If we don't confess Jesus Christ as Lord, if we don't embrace him by faith, then we will be punished on the last day. The wrath of God we have racked up because of our sins will fall on us and crush us.

Fourth, we respond in worship. Religious people cannot worship because they feel like it's owed to them. They are too good to need God. But people who have confessed their sin and been forgiven by God will naturally respond with worship.

> **But I with the voice of thanksgiving will sacrifice to you; what I have vowed I will pay. Salvation belongs to the LORD!** (2:9)

This is worship! During the reformation the reformers said, "Soli Deo gloria" (glory to God alone). Salvation belongs to God. I have nothing. I can't save myself. I'm swallowed up. There's nothing I can do to earn it. God is gracious!

Did you notice that Jonah doesn't tell God what to do? He surrenders control and worships. I think that's a mark of true prayer. Prayer is saying, "God, You change me. Change what I'm thinking and my will. I'm not going to give You any "ifs"; there are no deals here, I just want what you want." True prayer is a complete and total resignation of my will to God's will. Jonah experiences an internal change, but his circumstances haven't changed. It is after this change in Jonah that God changes his situation.

> **And the LORD spoke to the fish, and it vomited Jonah out upon the dry land. Then the word of the LORD came to Jonah the second time, saying, "Arise, go to Nineveh."** (2:10-3:2a)

After having this wonderful time of worship, Jonah thanks God for being so gracious and loving to him. But then God responds by telling Jonah that he still needs to do the first thing and preach to Nineveh. God did not let Jonah get away from being obedient, and He will not let you get away either.

God will accomplish His will for you whether it's forgiving your spouse or going to Nineveh. You're not getting around it, and He's not changing His mind. You ran from God because you didn't want to do it, but now God has brought you back, and now it's time to deal with the first issue. The good news is that Jonah changed, and we can too. You see, we know that Jonah's prayer was real because he didn't pray to change God; rather, after praying he was changed by God so that he obeyed God. This time when God told Jonah to preach to the Ninevites, Jonah did it. But can the same be said of you?

Where are you at with God right now? Honestly, where are you at with God? Are you suffering? Do you need grace? Are you running from Him? Are you trying to plug your ears and disobey what He's telling you to do?

I want to encourage us to go back to the psalms and let God through His word shape our prayer life to this honest, real style of prayer. In this place we're not afraid to admit our shortcomings; we're not afraid to admit that we're idolaters because we know Jesus is full of grace. Is this what your prayer life looks like? Are you pulling up the gracious promises of God through faith, like Jonah, and experiencing a deeper communion and relationship with God? I believe God can do this in us.

Paul Miller says, "If you're not praying then you are quietly confident that time, money, and talent are all you need in life. You'll always be a little too tired, a little too busy. But if, like Jesus, you realize you can't do life on your own, then no matter how busy, no matter how tired you are, you will always find the time to pray."[12]

I pray that you hear this. It's not through religion or being a better person that God will love you. The gospel is that Jesus, though perfect, took on your sins and died for you. If you embrace Him by faith then all of His righteousness, all of His goodness, and the love of the Father is credited to you. For those who have wandered back into religion, I pray that your prayer life would go to a deeper level like Jonah's, and like Jonah you could experience the grace of God even in your darkest moments.

HOW TO CHANGE A CITY

Then the word of the LORD came to Jonah the second time, saying, "Arise, go to Nineveh, that great city, and call out against it the message that I tell you." So Jonah arose and went to Nineveh, according to the word of the LORD. Now Nineveh was an exceedingly great city, three days' journey in breadth.

Jonah began to go on the city, going a day's journey. And he called out, "Yet forty days, and Nineveh shall be overthrown!" And the people of Nineveh believed God. They called for a fast and put on sackcloth, from the greatest of them to the least of them. The word reached the king of Nineveh, and he arose from his throne, removed his robe, covered himself with sackcloth, and sat in ashes.

And he issued a proclamation and published through Nineveh, "By the decree of the king and his nobles: let neither man nor beast, herd nor flock, taste anything. Let them not feed or drink water, but let man and beast be covered with sackcloth, and let them call out mightily to God. Let everyone turn from his evil way and from the violence that is in his hands. Who knows? God may turn and relent and turn from his fierce anger, so that we may not perish."

When God saw what they did, how they turned from their evil way, God relented of the disaster that he had said he would do to them, and he did not do it.

—Jonah 3

Have you ever given thought to what the God of the Bible is like? What are His attributes? What is His nature? A.W. Tozer once said, "What comes into our minds when we think about God is the most important thing about us."[13] Our lives and our desires are directed by the image we have in our mind of who God is. If we think God is cruel, we will either fear Him or flee from Him, but we'll never love Him. Jesus says the greatest commandment is to "love the LORD your God with all your heart and with all your soul and with all your strength and with all your mind" (Luke 10:27). This is troublesome, however, if the only image we have of God is one that invokes fear. If you want to get into heaven, you need to realize that the only people in heaven are those who love God and want to be with God. Some of us think that God is this Being out in the cosmos searching the earth in order to bless good little boys and girls with prosperity, comfort, and the American dream. If we live this way, we will spend all of our days trying really hard to earn God's favor but only be interested in what He can give us, not in His heart. We won't love Him. We'll only want a good life.

What we need is a clearer picture of God. Fortunately, Jonah 3 can help us.

This passage of scripture is going to show us that God is (at least) three things: He's 1) sovereign, 2) gracious, and 3) on a mission.

First, when I refer to God as a sovereign God, what I mean is that God is in absolute, complete, and total control of everything in the Universe. One hundred percent. Psalm 115:3

explains it this way: "Our God is in the heavens; he does all that he pleases." Also, Psalm 24:1 says this: "The earth is the LORD's and the fullness thereof." He made it; He owns it. God is the sovereign king of the universe. All things in the world, even the people who inhabit the world, belong to God; they're under His ownership. He's the sovereign king over all. Everything we see was made by His word, is held together by His power, and exists for His glory.

All of creation does exactly what God wants them to do, except mankind. In the Garden of Eden, Adam and Eve, representing mankind, pushed away from God and chose to rebel. Because of their sin, we are all rebels, or as R. C. Sproul says, "In the slightest act of rebellion we commit cosmic treason,"[14] and we desire to live for our own glory. We've seen this in Jonah. The wind, the waves, and the fish all obey the voice of the Lord, but Jonah runs. Everything in creation obeys God perfectly, but Jonah is on the run. This is where the sovereignty of God might shock us. Even mankind's rebellion is under the sovereignty of God. God uses our rebellion to actually show us His graciousness when we deserve His wrath. If we cannot see that we are rebellious and deserving of His wrath, we will never see His grace. God even used our rebelliousness to nail His Son to a wooden cross so that we could see His love demonstrated for us in real life.

Jonah deserves a divine beating for running from God. If your kid bolts into the street where cars are flying by, you are going to quickly grab their arm and yank them back to safety. Very few parents say, "Uh oh! Baby, come back over here." No, there will be discipline. First of all, they scared mama to death. Second, they were disobedient. They've been taught not to run into the street, but they did it anyway. As a parent, I can tell you it feels incredibly intense to have your child disobey like that. Why would we expect God to feel differently? Rather, we should expect God to come down hard on Jonah for his disobedience.

But that is not what God does. God pursues him and captures his heart again and gives him grace. When writing to the Ephesians about the sovereignty and graciousness of God, the apostle Paul says, "Blessed be the God and Father of our Lord Jesus Christ, who has blessed us in Christ with every spiritual blessing in the heavenly places, even as he chose us in him before the foundation of the world, that we should be holy and blameless before him. In love he predestined us for adoption as sons through Jesus Christ, according to the purpose of his will" (Eph. 1:3-5).

What does that mean, "according to the purpose of his will?" It means that God is sovereign. When God makes a decision He discusses it amongst Himself. Father, Son, and Holy Spirit. He goes to His own counsel. He doesn't go to human beings or creation for help. The council has its own will "to the praise of his glorious grace."

Second, God is gracious. Why does He choose people from the foundation of the world? Why does He predestine people to believe in Jesus Christ by His own council to the praise of His glorious grace? It is so that people would follow the thread of His sovereignty up to an enormous, incredible, gracious God. Paul goes on to say,

> To the praise of his glorious grace, with which he has blessed us in the Beloved. In him we have redemption through his blood, the forgiveness of our trespasses, according to the riches of his grace, which he has lavished upon us, in all wisdom and insight making known to us the mystery of his will, according to his purpose which he set forth in Christ as a plan for the fullness of time, to unite all things in him, things in heaven and things on earth. (Eph. 1:6-10)

God has sovereignly predestined us. This means sinners received grace through faith for adoption so that we would praise God's glorious grace. What does that mean? If I think that God has accepted and adopted me because I pulled myself up by the bootstraps, I will praise my own efforts.

This does not cause us to chase that thread up to the grace of God, only the sovereign action of God does. Only seeing that we do not deserve anything but wrath (just like Jonah) is what turns our eyes to God.

Grace is what causes us to love God. We are enemies of God until He adopts us and brings us from life to death. Grace is what creates love and praise and joy in our hearts. Grace is what leads us to do all things for the glory of God. This leads us to the third thing about God.

Third, God is missional. He's on a transformational mission. In Ephesians, He's on a mission to unite all things for the praise of His grace. He's set on renewing all of creation for His own glory. In the book of Jonah, God is giving us a picture of how His mission renews a city—and not just any city, but Nineveh, the biggest, baddest, most metropolitan city in the world. It took three days to walk through the city of Nineveh. It doesn't even take three days to walk through New York City. This is a big city. It's busy. There's a lot going on. When God wants to show the world how sovereign and gracious He is, he chooses Nineveh. I don't think there would be any city in current times that could prove God's sovereignty in His graciousness more than Nineveh's modern-day equivalent, Mosul, Iraq. God chose Nineveh—the sworn enemy of Israel!

These people are imperialistic conquerors, and Jonah is disgusted by them. If God can change a city like Nineveh, what can He do in your city? This story should fill us with great hope, purpose, and excitement for the future of our cities, because God loves cities! Why? It is because people are made in the image of God, the *imago dei*, and there is more *imago dei* per square inch in the city than in the country.

God pursues people in cities. We see the apostle Paul in the Book of Acts going from city to city to plant churches. But, how does God go about changing an entire city? If you've been around the church for a while, the word "revival" likely comes to mind. What does a revival look like? I grew up in a church that loved revivals. For some reason the churches I grew up in thought they could plan revivals. But you can't really do that.

The type of revival or renewal that we're talking about is when a lot of people come to faith during a short time period. The people in a city determine the culture of a city. As people come to faith, and then those people take their faith with them wherever they go, the culture of a city begins to change. Business owners begin to run their companies with a different set of ethics and principles; they let the gospel shape their business practices. No longer are they controlled by the bottom line, but they share their profits with those less fortunate. They train people less fortunate and help them succeed. The same goes for every public arena in a city: politics, government, social services, whatever it is. God changes people through grace, and the people transform the city through grace; that's revival. God does a work in their hearts, and then they take that work to their city.

But you can't plan a revival because it's not done by man. We don't save ourselves, and we don't change our own hearts. Only the Spirit does that; God orchestrates it. When God wants to change a city, he starts by changing a man. Alan Redpath says this: "When God wants to do an impossible task, He takes an impossible man and crushes him."[15] That's what He has done with Jonah. Jonah was a good old religious boy, very moral, buttoned up tight, voted red—that's Jonah, conservative as they get. But Jonah had forgotten the depths of his sinfulness;

he began to feel superior to others. He looked down on the Ninevites.

When God commanded Jonah to go to the Ninevites, he left in the opposite direction. He couldn't do it. The Ninevites were just too bad in his mind, too liberal, too immoral. There was no way Jonah was going to go to Nineveh and offer them the free gift of salvation and adoption into the family of God. He probably thought something like, "God can't adopt people like that. No. They're too bad. They're too dirty, too sinful, too wicked, too bent. God can't have people like that in His family around His table, eating at His dinner. No. I won't have it."

But God orchestrates all of creation to bring about what Keller calls "an explosion of grace" in Jonah's life.[16] The crazy thing is this is a guy who has already been adopted and brought in! This same Jonah needed another explosion of grace in order to be sent out on this mission to bring the gospel to the Ninevites.

Go back through the first two chapters of the book of Jonah, and look for how many times the author writes the word "down." Jonah goes *down* to Nineveh, *down* to get in a boat, *down* in the bottom of a boat; he's thrown overboard and goes *down* to the depths of the sea.

The author is brilliant! He's telling us when we're running from God, the trajectory is *down, down, down, down,* but then at the end of chapter 2 we see Jonah begin to rise through repentance. He is finally able to see and confess his sin. When Jonah receives the grace of God, we see him rise, rise, rise, and rise, which culminates when he looks to the temple, seeing the sacrifice that represents Jesus Christ who paid the price for sinners. He has a grace explosion and worships the Lord of salvation. But then the whale vomits him out upon the shore! I love this! At this point we might think the story is over. The End. But it's not over yet.

He's been delivered, he's been rescued, and God has clearly been gracious to him, but God is not gracious for gracious' sake. God is on a mission. He barely let Jonah get the water out of his lungs and unwind the seaweed from around his neck before addressing him for the second time: "Go preach to the Ninevites." This time, miraculously, thankfully, Jonah obeys.

One time when I was a kid, my brother and I decided to blow something up (which was a common occurrence in our house). We made this thing called "the works bomb." Basically you put this—I probably shouldn't say this. It's a good way to get arrested. I found that out the hard way. Okay, well, you take this bottle and put in this certain chemical, then some aluminum foil, and then you shake it up in a two-liter bottle and throw it. Of course, being a kid, playing with "the works bomb" escalated to blowing up my neighbor's mailbox, and I got arrested. But let's redeem this illustration.

Just like our little two-ingredient "works bomb" produced a great explosion, so there are really only two ingredients involved in an explosion of grace in a person's life. We see these ingredients come together while Jonah is in the belly of the whale. The first ingredient is that we have to become what we despise. We watched Jonah go through this painfully stunning awakening when he realized he was just like the Ninevites. The second ingredient is that we have to trust the sacrifice. After becoming who he despised, Jonah remembered the sacrifice. He looked toward the temple, the altar and the sacrifice—the Old Testament version of trusting Jesus—and he believed.

That's it! Two ingredients: I'm a sinner, but there has been a sacrifice. I'm a sinner, yet Jesus Christ was better. Jesus is the only man who has ever lived who didn't need grace. Jesus was perfect. He was sinless. But Jesus didn't use His sinlessness for

His own benefit. He could've been the most powerful ruler. He could've been the biggest Don the world has ever seen, but instead, Jesus became our sacrifice. Jesus took our place.

You will know you've experienced grace when you look upon your enemy and see yourself. You no longer see addicts or beggars; you see yourself. That is how you know you have a transformed heart: you see someone running from God and instead of thinking you are better than them, you search your own heart for where you are running. This is how God changes a city. He first changes one man.

Have you been changed like this? Have you experienced this type of explosion of grace? I'm not asking if you are religious. I'm not asking if you believe the Ten Commandments. I'm not even asking how well you follow those commandments; I'm asking if your heart has been shaped by grace.

Here's how you can know if you have been changed by grace. A grace explosion does two things: it 1) saves us, and 2) sanctifies us. What does that mean? When God saves you, He saves you for a purpose; there is a mission you are being drafted into. Every single Christian who's put their faith in the grace of God and faith in Jesus Christ has been made into a missionary. How well you respond to that calling shows how responsive you are to the grace of God. Jonah shows us the evidence that a grace explosion can have upon each of us. God will send you on a mission with His message as His missionary to take the gospel to people who are far from grace so that they can come to know this sovereign, gracious, missional God who has loved them from all eternity. He sent His own Son as a missionary to collect us into the family of God.

Now, I know what you're thinking. "I can't remember all the details of the gospel. I am not a gifted orator. I don't think I could explain the gospel to others." But neither could Jonah!

So Jonah arose and went to Nineveh, according to the word of the LORD. Now Nineveh was an exceedingly great city, three days' journey in breadth. Jonah began to go into the city, going a day's journey. And he called out, "Yet forty days, and Nineveh shall be overthrown!" (3:3-4)

It is a big deal that Jonah is in Nineveh. He is now in a territory he shouldn't be in; he's going to a place that only a missionary would dare go. It's not safe and he could be killed. He's going into a hotbed of animosity to inform a polytheistic culture that they have offended Yahweh, the covenant God of Israel. Even worse, he tells them God's going to come and destroy them all. It is just unbelievable how God uses our feeble efforts. It's never our cleverness or knowledge that brings people to Jesus; it doesn't work that way. God is the one who works in the hearts of people. We're faithful and He makes us fruitful. What happens next is nuts.

And the people of Nineveh believed God. They called for a fast and put on sackcloth, from the greatest of them to the least of them. (3:5)

What? Over and over throughout this story, the people far from God believe while the religious man runs! The religious guy runs and doesn't believe God, and now the whole city of Nineveh believes and repents. They put on sackcloth, which is a sign of mourning and repentance. This rebellious city has responded to the grace of God by mourning their sin and asking for forgiveness.

Now, this is revival! This is a supernatural act of God. I can imagine Jonah. His theology just got flipped upside down. There was no pleading or emotional manipulation. But the sovereign, gracious, missional God chose to grant repentance to the people of Nineveh. We see this also in the thirteenth chapter of the Book of Acts when some Gentiles heard the gospel: "They began rejoicing and glorifying the word of the Lord, and as many as were appointed to eternal life believed (Acts 13:48).

The sovereign God appoints some people to believe the gospel and repent. This is simply a gift of God. Citywide renewal happened because God changed one man.

I'd like to speak to two groups of people: the first group is made up of those who are far from God, who live outside the grace of God. For those who have never believed in the grace of God, let me tell you, He can give you a new family. Some people have never experienced that. Some people have been religious their whole life but may have never met Jesus Christ as their Lord and Savior.

Then there's a second group of people, the ones who know Jesus Christ intimately, have been forgiven of their sins, but are not living on mission. It's been a long time since they've had an explosion of grace in their hearts, and they don't truly understand that to be a Christian means to be a missionary.

When we're saved, we go on mission with Jesus. We should take the gospel to our friends, neighbors, and family members and watch God do the miraculous.

I know if you're a Christian, you have likely sat through arm-twisting, manipulative sermons that make you feel guilty about not being on mission. This is not what being on mission is about. This is about a gracious and sovereign God who's on mission inviting you into His redemptive mission for the world. Here are three simple truths from this text and the Gospel that changes how we do mission.

First is justification. Justification means we are already made right with God because of Jesus' work and mission. He's saved you and me. We were enemies of God but now we are His friends. Jesus, the perfect missionary, has already performed perfectly for us so we don't have to be all-stars. Our righteousness isn't found in being a missionary. Our justification, our being made right with God, is not found in being good missionaries. We are made right with God because of the work of Jesus. There is no earning it. If you feel there's guilt or shame for being a bad missionary, which some of us are, know that Jesus realized this about us and died for us while we were yet sinners!

Second is sanctification. Sanctification is the process of us being made into the image of Jesus. In other words, and in relation to mission, we should be growing toward being better missionaries. We should be growing more confident in sharing our faith, have more ease in loving our neighbors, and sacrifice more for our family. In justification you've been delivered from sin, but in sanctification you've been set free from the slavery of sin, not just the penalty of sin. In sanctification, we've been set free from the power of sin and can now resist sin. Because of this I can also resist the temptation to be overly selfish by hiding in my garage and instead go hang out with my neighbor across the street. That's what it means to be a Christian. We've been set free from the penalty of sin and the power of sin. Does it mean I'm going to be perfect? Absolutely not. Does it mean I can resist sin? Absolutely.

How else are we going to show our neighbor who God is and what He's like? I might get in trouble for saying this, but for many of us, the most God-honoring, missional thing we could do is have a beer with our neighbor. Take the Jesus pin off, put it on the nightstand, and go have a real conversation with a real human being who needs the grace of God just as much as you need the grace of God. If you feel opposed to that, I would challenge you by asking, "What is the gospel doing in your life? How is your heart not broken for your neighbor? Are you so afraid you're going to be corrupted by one sip of alcohol or lose the reputation of a nice, clean, religious person?"

Christ says there is nothing we can take into our bodies that corrupts our heart, nothing (Acts 7:15). We're corrupted by what comes out of the heart. Religion, moralism, pride—that's what corrupts us. Listen, it's hard to say stuff like that, but I think it's worth saying. We've been justified, set free completely from the penalty of sin. We're never going to be judged again. Christians are never going to be judged again because Christ was judged for us.

We've been set free from the power of sin. We're not slaves to sin anymore. I can have a beer and not get drunk. I can have a sip of whiskey and a cigar and not get drunk. You're not losing your testimony by doing that. You're losing your testimony by hiding in the basement and watching Left Behind. You're not on mission. God sends us to our enemies. God sends us to the broken. He saves us so He can send us. Tim Keller says, "God is a spiritual tornado. He never sucks us in without sending us out."[17] If you're saved, you're sent on mission.

Third, as Christians, God fills us with His Spirit. What does that mean? It means you're never alone again. You're never powerless again. You never have to walk into a Starbucks and think, "Could I really share my faith? Could God really save this person through one sentence? Could God really change my neighbor?" You're never powerless again. For Jonah, the Holy Spirit took one sentence, "God's going to kill you," and through it the whole city was saved and changed. It is amazing what God can do in our lives if we actually listen to the Spirit and attempt something for God.

If you call yourself a Christian and can't remember the last time you talked to an outsider about the gospel, you're like Jonah, and you need an explosion of grace in your life. You need a personal revival. You need an explosion of grace to give you a deeper awareness of your own sinfulness and an even greater awareness of God's grace. God has strategically and sovereignly placed people in your life so that your story and relationship can be impacted for Jesus.

By grace, choose not to stay home on the couch or in the garage! You have been justified. You have been sanctified. You are filled with the Holy Spirit and called to be on mission. Go to your Nineveh.

Thankfully, Jesus is the perfect missionary we fail to be. Jesus' obedience did not just save a city like Nineveh but saves anyone who puts their faith in Him.

ANGRY ENOUGH TO DIE

Then the word of the LORD came to Jonah the second time, saying, "Arise, go to Nineveh, that great city, and call out against it the message that I tell you." So Jonah arose and went to Nineveh, according to the word of the LORD. Now Nineveh was an exceedingly great city, three days' journey in breadth. Jonah began to go into the city, going a day's journey. And he called out, "Yet forty days, and Nineveh shall be overthrown!" And the people of Nineveh believed God. They called for a fast and put on sackcloth, from the greatest of them to the least of them....

When God saw what they did, how they turned from their evil way, God relented of the disaster that he had said he would do to them, and he did not do it.

But it displeased Jonah exceedingly, and he was angry. And he prayed to the LORD and said, "O LORD, is not this what I said when I was yet in my country? That is why I made haste to flee to Tarshish; for I knew that you are a gracious God and merciful, slow to anger and abounding in steadfast love, and relenting from disaster. Therefore now, O LORD, please take my life from me, for it is better for me to die than to live." And the LORD said, "Do you do well to be angry?"

Jonah went out of the city and sat to the east of the city and made a booth for himself there. He sat under it in the shade, till he should see what would become of the city. Now the LORD God appointed a plant and made it come up over Jonah, that it might be a shade over his head, to save him from his discomfort. So Jonah was exceedingly glad because of the plant. But when dawn came up the next day, God appointed a worm that attacked the plant, so that it withered. When the sun rose, God appointed a scorching east wind, and the sun beat down on the head of Jonah so that he was faint. And he asked that he might die and said, "It is better for me to die than to live." But God said to Jonah, "Do you do well to be angry for the plant?" And he said, "Yes, I do well to be angry, angry enough to die." And the LORD said, "You pity the plant, for which you did not labor, nor did you make it grow, which came into being in a night and perished in a night. And should not I pity Nineveh, that great city, in which there are more than 120,000 persons who do not know their right hand from their left, and also much cattle?"

—Jonah 3:1-5, 10 and 4:1-11

John Calvin has famously said, "Hence we may infer, that the human mind is, so to speak, a perpetual forge of idols."[18] We take good things from God, turn them into God things, and when a good thing becomes a God thing, it becomes a bad thing. What happens is that we take these good things, created things, and we worship them. We look to them to find fulfillment in life. We depend upon them for our happiness. "Once I get [blank], then I'll finally be happy."

This is something we learned in Jonah 2:8. Unbeknownst to us, when we worship idols, we forsake the hope of steadfast love, or as another translation says, we forsake grace. When we worship an idol and not the true God, we miss out on grace.

Most of the time we are not aware that we are doing this. Very few of us have little wooden idols at home that we bow down to and worship, but we do have other idols. When the prophet Ezekiel talks about idols, he says that they are in the heart (Ez. 20:16). Once you understand that the biblical concept of idolatry includes heart level desires, you realize idolatry doesn't have to actually be things like your car or your TV or your sports team. It can be, but most of the time it's something in our heart that we rely on for our identity more than God. And when we are relying on something other than God to give us an identity and then our identity gets threatened, we freak out.

That's why we get anxious, or fearful, or angry: an idol is being threatened. That's why we get stressed out and despair. It's idolatry. Let's take a closer look at what the Bible says about idolatry. If you broke the Bible up into four chapters, you would get something like this: Chapter One: Creation; Chapter Two: Fall; Chapter Three: Redemption; Chapter Four: New Creation.

CHAPTER ONE: CREATION

God is the uncreated Creator. He's the reason for everything. He's the meaning behind it all: the source of all joy, all comfort, all peace, and all satisfaction. God created it all, and is the source of it all. In Him, you find everything that you need. Everything was created for His own glory.

CHAPTER TWO: FALL

Adam and Eve, the first humans, rebelled against God's righteous rule and fatherly care. They decided to strike out on their own, and that went really bad for them. They fell from grace. They were punished and cursed for their cosmic treason, and all of creation was cursed along with it. This means that mankind was cut off from God; we became separated from Him and from His glory. Forsaking God created a vacuum in the human soul that needs to be filled. We long for God and His glory but can never get back to him on our own. Because of this we try to use created things to fill that vacuum, and that is idolatry.

CHAPTER THREE: REDEMPTION

Although God cursed all of creation for Adam and Eve's rebellion, He promised to send a man who would redeem everything, who would crush the head of the serpent and bring people and creation back into a right relationship with Him and each other. We see glimpses of this promised redemption all through the Old Testament in the covenants, the temple and the sacrificial system, and in many stories, including Jonah. Jesus accomplishes redemption when He enters the world, lives a perfect life, dies a substitutionary death on the cross, and is resurrected three days later, defeating death and therefore reuniting man to God.

CHAPTER FOUR: NEW CREATION

Jesus' work on the cross makes sinners right with God, but it also guarantees the redemption of the whole world. This is the new heaven and the new earth. Jesus is making all things new right now. The new heaven and the new earth will be the world that we have always wanted. Jesus right now is ushering His people and all of creation into a new eternity where everything will be as it should be. We will have everything we look for and everything we want: prosperity, health, laughter, joy, Alabama football, increasing love, and the knowledge of God. Increasing happiness day after day in the new creation—that's where we're heading.

That's the story of the Bible. God created everything perfect; we rebelled against God, Jesus redeemed us to God, and He is ushering in a new reality. It's the best story that's ever been told. It's what all of our stories should point toward. No matter how bad things have been in your life, no matter how dark, no matter how abusive, no matter how despondent you've been—in Christ you will always have a glorious future awaiting you in the new heaven and new earth.

If you want this story to be your story, then you need to be in Christ. What do I mean by that? Everyone's story follows these four chapters to some degree. We were all created. As a baby it was good—no problems. But then, each and every one of us experienced some sort of fall. At some point we wake up and realize things are not so good. Some of us wake up sooner than others. We come to this sense that something is broken—that is the fall. Maybe it took you a few dodge balls to the face to realize you weren't as good at sports as your peers. Or you woke up and realized there are prettier girls than you. This is where we see, as John Calvin says, the idol factory of the human heart enter the picture. You become distraught, wondering what will make you feel right again. You ask, "What's going to make life good again or make me good again? What is going to get me out of this mess?" Jesus is not our first choice as a redeemer.

Those who find their identity in Christ look to Jesus for redemption. When they realize they don't feel pretty enough, smart enough, or good enough, they look to Jesus, and thank Him that He is their righteousness. But we don't do that naturally. We don't trust Jesus for our redemption most of the time. What do we do? We look for redemption in ourselves. You might not say it out loud, but on some level you're probably thinking, "I'm not pretty enough. I need new clothes and the right accessories; I need a makeover." Or, "I'm not athletic enough. I'll work twice as hard as the other guys and I'll prove that I'm good enough." Or, "I'm not happy with the way my life is going. I don't feel fulfilled. I will create my own world online. Video games, pornography, and social media are my way of feeling special." Whatever it is, we all use things to prop ourselves up as *the* redeemer so that we don't have to rely on God. We want to rule our life.

But we are not God. Theologian Chris Wright says, "False gods never fail to fail."[19] Jesus is the only God who can save us from what is really wrong with us. He is the only one who can give us what we all want: the new creation. Your attempts to save yourself will never usher in the new heaven and the new earth.

How do you find out if you're trusting in a substitute savior? This should be eye-opening for some of us. Some of us truly believe we trust Jesus and are a Christian. We believe we are following God.

Think hard, or maybe you don't have to. Maybe you already know. I guarantee that each person reading this book is somehow trusting in a substitute savior right now for peace, joy, and fulfillment. In order to better understand how we can identify these false saviors, let's get back to the book of Jonah to learn some diagnostic tools to help us.

There are two emotions in the book that reveal Jonah's idolatry: 1) anger, which leads to 2) despair. When your anger leads to despair, you know you're trusting in an idol for something that can be found only in Jesus.

But it displeased Jonah exceedingly and he was angry. (4:1)

Jonah has just finished preaching the worst gospel sermon of all time to the Ninevites. "In a few days, God is going to destroy you all." But then God does what only God can do; he changes the hearts of all the Ninevites in an instant—sovereign grace happened. They threw ashes on their heads, stripped down to their loincloths, and repented.

As Jonah walks away the whole city cries out for God to save them, "but it displeased Jonah exceedingly." Now, the Bible does not waste words. What it actually says in the Hebrew is that Jonah found it exceedingly evil, and he was angry.

If you know anything about the life of the prophets in the Old Testament, you know it's the job no one wants. They were normally commanded to tell God's people what they didn't want to hear, and hardly anyone listened to them. One of them walked around naked. Their job was just horrible.

Just imagine being Jeremiah, the weeper. You are preaching and everyone screams at you, "Shut up!" This is the glorified office of God's prophet. Jeremiah wept because the people didn't listen and were carried off to Babylon in bondage. Here in Jonah, we have one of the rare places where a prophet is actually heard and obeyed—it's a win. But Jonah doesn't appear to feel like a winner.

This doesn't even make sense to me! It's like me getting up to preach every Sunday at my church and being upset that people are coming to know Jesus for the first time. We get upset when we lose, but Jonah is upset that he's winning. This reveals something in his heart—he is calling evil what God calls good.

> **And he prayed to the LORD and said, "O LORD, is not this what I said when I was yet in my country? That is why I made haste to flee to Tarshish; for I knew that you were a gracious God and merciful, slow to anger and abounding in steadfast love, and relenting from disaster. (4:2)**

Anger is not sin, by the way. Scripture says, "Be angry and do not sin" (Eph. 4:26). To get angry is not sin. So, when you get angry, pray to the Lord. That's a good way to respond to your anger, and at first it looks like that's what Jonah is doing, but it's not.

Jonah is reflecting back to when the Lord first told him to go to Nineveh. He knew what would happen; he knew that God would be gracious to the Ninevites, and that's exactly why he didn't want to go in the first place. He's mad that God didn't smoke this whole town. Moralistic people love the story of Sodom and Gomorrah, and they pray for God to do it again.

"Hit Vegas, God!"

"Washington, D.C.? Yes! Smoke them out, LORD!"

We might think that about Mosul right now, but then we would be just like Jonah. Moralistic people don't want a loving God—they want a wrathful, vengeful, angry God who hates the people they hate. But Jonah is not just angry. It's worse than that.

> **Therefore now, O LORD, please take my life from me, for it is better for me to die than to live. (4:3)**

This is the kind of anger that leads to despair. Jonah is angry enough to die. He is so angry at what God is doing that he doesn't want to get up in the morning. It's important for us to see that his anger diagnoses his idolatry. Something other than God is at the center of his life. How do we know? Because Jonah believes God is wrong.

Jonah would rather have a tribal God. To bring it home for us, Jonah does not want Jesus as his redeemer. Jonah wants a way around Jesus. Jonah doesn't want grace. He wants a god that will do things the way he wants, a god that he can manage and control and manipulate. Jonah wants a safe God.

If you know anything about C.S. Lewis' *Chronicles of Narnia*, you know there is an allegory between Aslan and Jesus. At one point in the story, a number of children are being prepared by Mr. Beaver to meet Aslan, their Redeemer, for the first time, and they don't know that he's actually a lion.

"You'll understand when you see him."

"But shall we see him?" asked Susan."'Why, Daughter of Eve, that's what I brought you here for. I'm to lead you where you shall meet him,' said Mr. Beaver."

"Is—is he a man?" asked Lucy."'Aslan a man!' said Mr. Beaver sternly, 'Certainly not. I tell you he is the King of the wood and the son of the great Emperor-beyond-the-Sea. Don't you know who is the King of Beasts? Aslan is a lion—*the* Lion, the great Lion.'"

"'Ooh!' said Susan, 'I'd thought he was a man. Is he—quite safe? I shall feel rather nervous about meeting a lion.'"

"'That you will, dearie, make no mistake,' said Mrs. Beaver; 'if there's anyone who can appear before Aslan without their knees knocking, they're either braver than most or else just silly.'"

"'Then he isn't safe?' asked Lucy."'"Safe?' said Mr. Beaver; 'don't you hear what Mrs. Beaver tells you? Who said anything about safe? 'Course he isn't safe. But he's good. He's the king, I tell you.'"[20]

If your god is safe—he thinks like you, talks like you, acts like you—then you don't serve the real God. You serve a false god, a figment of your imagination. God is sovereign. His thoughts are above our thoughts. His ways are above our ways. If God does not cross your will often, then more than likely you have an idol.

There's a lot of research going around right now that says most Americans have done this exact thing. We've taken the untamed lion of scripture—Jesus, who rules from on high, who does what He pleases—and we've "tamed Him" to meet our moralistic, therapeutic deism.

This is what theologian David Wells says about our church culture:

> We have turned to a God that we can use rather than to a God we must obey; we have turned to a God who will fulfill our needs rather than to a God before whom we must surrender our rights to ourselves. He is a God for us, for our satisfaction—not because we have learned to think of him in this way through Christ but because we have learned to think of him this way through the marketplace…and we have come to assume that it must be so in the church as well. And so we transform the God of mercy into a God who is at our mercy. We imagine that he is benign and he will act as we act as we toy with his reality and co-opt with him in the promotion of our ventures and our careers.[21]

Instead of dealing with God as He is, we say, "I want a god who serves my needs," or, "I want a god who will give me my best life right now," or, "I want a god who will bless my business." Our hearts are idol factories. We want to create gods into our image instead of serving the One True God. We want to build our lives on something other than Jesus. But most of the time I don't think we are even aware of it. We read our Bible, pray, go to church, and might not even know how to diagnose the idolatry that's going on in our hearts. So, let me try to help you do a diagnostic right now.

What do you have in your life that, if it was taken from you, would cause you to run from God? If it was gone, would you be angry enough to die? Would you lie in bed until noon without a desire to get up even for your closest friends? If you have any self-awareness, you already know the answer. It could be your spouse, it could be kids, it could be money, but it can also be an idolatry of the heart. It could be comfort, it could be security, it could be peace, it could be power, it could be control—it could be all of these things.

What we're going to see is that when something comes between God and us, God gracefully goes to war with that thing. If you are a Christian, God isn't at war with you; He's at war with your idols. Because we can love "that thing" so much, it may feel like God is trying to hurt us, but He's not: He's trying to free us.

And the LORD said, "Do you do well to be angry?" (4:4)

Moralistic people like to point out the symptoms of others' idolatry. They'll confront and condemn outward bad behavior. "You are angry. Stop being angry! You are a fool. Stop being a fool!" But that's not how God responds, although it's true that Jonah is angry and a fool. Instead, God asks him a question. God wants Jonah to see what's going on inside of his own heart. Jonah is praying, and God is responding. God is answering him. God, the source of all life, all meaning, all purpose, all joy, all happiness, is speaking with him, but Jonah doesn't care.

This is a key to diagnosing idolatry: Jonah is looking at the face of God, the source of all life and all hope and all happiness, but is still feeling unsatisfied.

Think about it this way. You are dying of thirst in the desert and see a well. As you walk up to it and look down, you see beautiful, clear, sparkling water and say, "I don't like the color of this well. I hate this well. God, why did you give me this well? I want something different. I want a Coke." It sounds ridiculous, but this is what's happening in the story. God is everything Jonah wants. God is everything Jonah needs, but Jonah would rather have his way, his tribal god, and his idols than have true satisfaction, true comfort. Do you see what's going on here?

God has come between Jonah and his idol, and Jonah gets mad, real mad.

> **Jonah went out of the city and sat to the east of the city and made a booth for himself there. He sat under it in the shade, till he should see what would become of the city. (4:5)**

What's he doing? Jonah is running from God, again. Did God tell him to leave the city? The city repents; Jonah washes out and makes a little booth where he can sit and pout.

Jonah walks away from the source of all comfort and tries to find some comfort in a little booth he made in the desert. That is what idolatry does: it drives you to leave the comfort of the Almighty God, and you go find comfort in a 401(k). You leave the satisfaction in God and hope that you can make it on your own. You leave God and search for your comfort in some broken little booth of your own making.

For Jonah, his ethnicity, his morality, his feelings of superiority over the Ninevites were more central to his identity as a person than his relationship with God. We could say it like this: Jonah was more Jew than Christian. Many of us can be more American than Christian. If Jonah really believed that God was sovereign, and gracious, and slow to anger and abounding in steadfast love, then he would have trusted God no matter what happened. If Jonah really believed God, he could have said, "God, I trust You. I know what You have planned is best for the world, Your glory, and me. I can trust You no matter how my life is going, no matter what my bank account looks like, no matter what my boss says, no matter what my neighbor is doing, and no matter what's going on in my family. I can trust You because You're sovereign, gracious, and full of love." But he can't. So God steps in front of his idol.

Many of us think we are Christians. We're nice, moral, good people until God starts idol-blocking us. God steps in front of what we really want (reputation, control, comfort, power), and then we get angry enough to die.

One of my own heart idols is my reputation. I want other people to think highly of me. I want people to know how hardworking I am, how punctual and thoughtful I am. I just want people to think well of me. I know there are many of you out there who are like that. But here in the life of Jonah, we see that God is not okay with us serving idols. God, in His sovereign grace, goes to war with our idols, and He usually does that through very normal and frustrating means.

When I moved to Omaha to begin a Church Planting Residency with the Acts 29 network, God went to war with my idols. I was addicted to approval and a slave to my reputation, and God loved me too much to let me stay that way. While in Omaha, I made an appointment with Acts 29 Pastor Bob Thune. I really respect Bob. He's a man of deep character. He's a brilliant theologian, and he's planted a wonderful, gospel-centered church. I was excited to meet with him, so we set a date and time.

The day of my meeting, my wife asked me to run an errand for her, and I completely lost track of time. I was clear across town when my phone sent me a 15-minute alert to meet with Bob. I panicked.

Now, back then I used to think that people who were late were irresponsible and bad planners who were unfit to lead. It had been years since I was late to a meeting, and I took great pride in that fact. For me, "on time" meant fifteen minutes early. I decided, "I can make it." I found the address, put it in my iPhone, and was weaving in and out of traffic to get there as fast as I could. Suddenly, I pulled up to the place, but it looked nothing like a church. I looked at my phone and realized that

I had typed in the wrong address. So, I put in the new address and routed it. My GPS then said it would take me 35 minutes to get there! Noooooooooo!

I went berserk, all by myself, beating the steering wheel and screaming. Eventually, I proceeded on the drive of shame. By the time I got there, not only was I late to a meeting, but I was also 45 minutes late to a meeting with a guy who was going to be my mentor! I was convinced he was judging me hard and thinking, "This guy can't be a church planter. He can't even show up to a meeting on time. Who does this guy think he is? He probably doesn't respect my time at all."

Feeling full of shame, I walked in. But Bob didn't shame me; he gave me a lot of grace. In that moment God showed me that my identity was wrapped up in what Bob thought of me. When my performance and reputation were challenged, I fell apart.

Here is what God revealed to me through that lesson. If my identity is something other than Jesus Christ, then it will never be safe. One missed appointment sent my identity as a leader into a downward spiral that left me feeling ashamed at my outburst of anger. But when my identity is secure in Christ, I can admit my failures without them crushing me because the gospel tells me that I'm already a failure.

Do you know the gospel tells you that? The cross proves you're a failure. You can't save yourself. You can never be good enough. You can never be smart enough. You can never be on time enough. You can never be a solid enough leader or a good enough parent or a good enough spouse. You are a failure. The cross proves this while simultaneously saying you are ridiculously loved. In the midst of your failure, you're loved. When I was at my lowest, beating the steering wheel like a fool, Jesus was at His best, loving me through it. Jesus loved you so much that He willingly went to the cross for you, despite your failures.

In that moment, I was so mad because I couldn't save myself. My self-salvation project failed me. I was late; therefore, I was no longer a good leader, I was no longer a good man, and I was no longer a church-planting prospect. I was crushed, despondent, and angry enough to die.

The LORD God appointed a plant… (4:6)

Earlier I mentioned an idea called moralistic therapeutic deism. This is the idea that there's a god out there that does everything that we want and serves us only. He's only there when we really need Him. It's like a doctor; you only go to a doctor when you're in need. Most of us live with this deistic idea of god. What is a deistic idea of God? It believes that God winds up the universe, sets it on a shelf, and sits back watching while it runs. Plants grow without His involvement, the planets do their thing, and the weather happens. That is a deistic understanding of the world, but not a biblical understanding. That is not a God-centered understanding. G. K. Chesterton said, "It is possible that God says every morning, 'Do it again' to the sun."[22] In a sense, this story would align with that. God speaks to a plant, and it obeys.

Jonah's out there in his little man-made booth trying to find his comfort away from God; he's really hot, so God appoints a plant to grow up over his head. Look what happens next.

> **Now the LORD God appointed a plant and made it come up over Jonah, that it might be a shade over his head, to save him from his discomfort. So Jonah was exceedingly glad because of the plant. (4:6)**

What a kind and gracious God, full of mercy and steadfast love. God's rebellious prophet runs away from the city and becomes mad at God; but Jonah's hot and thirsty, so God graciously gives him a plant for shade. This made Jonah "exceedingly glad."What is interesting here is that Jonah did not see this plant as an evidence of grace. Why isn't he thanking God for this thing God's created? Jonah does not thank God for the plant or recognize that He is the giver of all good things. What Jonah does is fall back into worshiping a created thing.

> **But when the dawn came up the next day, God appointed a worm that attacked the plant, so that it withered.** (4:7)

So, God first appointed a plant and now a worm—this is crazy. The sovereign God of the universe is even in control of worms! He might even have called the worm by name! God gives the worm the okay and it devours the plant. This is brilliant.

> **When the sun rose, God appointed a scorching east wind, and the sun beat down on the head of Jonah so that he was faint. And he asked that he might die and said, "It's better for me to die than to live."** (4:8)

Here we go again. Jonah tried to find comfort by running away from God, but that didn't work and God put him in the whale. Now, he is trying to find comfort out in the desert in his little booth, but that doesn't work either, so God gives him a plant. Now comes a scorching wind. This is God idol-blocking Jonah. Jonah is so frustrated with God because He is not doing things the way Jonah wants.

God is taking away all the props that Jonah has to stand on. What does God want him to do? God wants Jonah to look to Him for his comfort instead of going to these various created things.

Isn't this what we do? When things aren't going well, we run to some created thing. I have a friend who, when things aren't going well at home, runs to his work. Why? Because he feels like he can manage his work; he feels successful there. Work is easy compared to being a dad and husband. That's the definition of escapism, and thankfully God will not let His people do it. He cares about them too much to leave them alone.

Friend, listen to me. Why is God beating on this idolatry thing so much? It is because anything and everything except God in your life can be and will be taken from you. Your health could go in a second, your strength could be gone tomorrow—we all are just one doctor's report away from a terminal illness. Your marriage could go. One car accident and your kids could be gone. Anything other than God that you build your life on could be taken from you in an instant, and God is trying to show you through Jonah that idols never fail to fail.

> **But God said to Jonah, "Do you do well to be angry for the plant?" And he said, "Yes, I do well to be angry, angry enough to die." (4:9)**

This is how you know you're idol crazy. His anger isn't righteous or appropriate anger; it's anger that leads to despair. With the source of all things in front of him, he doubles down on his stupidity: "Yes, I do well to be angry, angry enough to die!"

Anger that leads to despair is like an alarm system that God has put in our heart to awaken us to the fact that we're forgetting the gospel. That we're looking to something other than Jesus to save us from our problems. It could be work, it could be video games, it could be hunting, or it could be Pinterest. Whatever you run to is your god.

> **And the LORD said, "You pity the plant, for which you did not labor, nor did you make it grow, which came into being in a night and perished in a night. And should not I pity Nineveh, that great city, in which there are more than 120,000 persons who do not know their right hand from their left, and also much cattle?" (4:10-11)**

Jonah's more upset about a plant, his idol, than about the Ninevites getting grace. God essentially tells Jonah, "You are angry at the wrong thing. You're not angry about what makes Me angry. This is about you and your plan. You want them to die; I want to give them grace."

I think it's pretty easy for us to live that way. We can live in our homes and neighborhoods far more concerned with our own personal comfort than God's plan for the renewal of our cities. We may think, "I need you to help me raise my kids, God. I got a whole lot of crazy in my house; I need help. Just forget about the city and help me!" But God didn't deal with Jonah that way, and He won't with us either. God rebuked Jonah for his selfishness and that was it. The End.

What an ending. The hero fails. The good guy is exposed as a religious bigot and then the credits roll. No redemption. No reconciliation. No restoration. No happily ever after. No new heaven and new earth. I've always hated this kind of ending because I want things to be fixed in the end. I think we're all hardwired by God for hope for the new heaven and the new earth where everything will be made right.

If God has wired us to hope in a better world, why would God (who wrote the story of creation, fall, redemption, restoration) end a book like this? You were probably taught in church as a kid that Jonah was the hero of this book. He's not. You might have heard something like, "Jonah disobeys,

God uses a whale to change Jonah's mind, and then Jonah obeys God. Alright, kids, go be like Jonah." But that's not what happens.

We're not meant to look at this story, nor any story in the Old Testament, and idolize the characters. They are not heroes. If Jonah were a hero, then his story would teach us salvation by works. That's religion. That's moralism. That is not the gospel. We're supposed to read this story and think that God is gracious. Jonah is an idolizing fool, just like me. Jonah's only hope, and my only hope, is the grace of God.

Jonah is clearly not the hero, but the Bible does tell us who the hero is in Matthew 12:38-41:

> Then some of the scribes and Pharisees answered him saying, "Teacher, we wish to see a sign from you," but Jesus answered them, "An evil and adulterous generation seeks for a sign, but no sign will be given to it except the sign of the prophet Jonah, for just as Jonah was three days and three nights in the belly of the great fish, so will the Son of Man be three days and three nights in the heart of the earth." The men of Nineveh will rise up at the judgment with this generation and condemn it, for they repented at the preaching of Jonah, and behold, something greater than Jonah is here.

Jesus finishes the story for us; He is the happily ever after that we don't get in Jonah. Jesus is the better Jonah. Jesus didn't run from God's call to be a missionary. Jesus left His country and came willingly. Jesus didn't get thrown into the wrath of God like Jonah because of His own rebellion. Jesus walked into it willingly for us. Jesus didn't stand back and hope that those far from God would get what was coming to them. Jesus saw what was coming to us, the wrath of God, and got in between it and us. He took our place and took upon Himself the punishment that we all deserve.

This is the cure for our idolatry: look to Jesus. Jesus is our redeemer. Jesus is our rescuer. Jesus is our savior. Like God sent Jonah to Nineveh, God sent the true and better Jonah to this earth from heaven so that we might be saved.

Will you trust Him? Will you turn from the idols of your heart and turn to the only redeemer who can guarantee you the new heaven and new earth?

INTO THE WILD

The book of Jonah is about a man running from God; actually, it's about men and women running from God. We've seen there are two ways to run from God. There's the moral way to run from God where you try to be a really good person, and there's the rebellious way to run from God where you totally disregard the commands of God.

The Book of Jonah shows us that both types of people are actually running from grace because the way that God relates to the universe and human beings is through grace. Still, God calls us through Jonah's story to understand that He loves us and desires for us to draw near to Him through His son Jesus.

I believe that there is one last lesson for us to learn from the book of Jonah: we need to follow Jesus into the wild.

You see, Jonah knew about the love of God, but he couldn't believe it when it counted. He knew the correct Bible answers, but those answers didn't impact his heart, as they should have. Jonah knew the love of God theologically and intellectually, but not intimately and experientially.

If God's love is like an ocean, Jonah is standing on the shoreline with his feet in the water. He can see it, hear its power, and even feel it tickling his toes. But he's not submersed in it or overwhelmed by it.

Let me ask you this question: are you in a similar situation? If you know Christ, you have experienced the love of God at one time or another in your life and have become brand new. At one time you were submersed in the love of God; you felt waves of grace crashing over your head...but now you're numb to it. Your feet are on the shore with your toes barely in the water. When you hear people talk about God's love, it's almost blasé. It doesn't warm your heart or move you to compassion. It doesn't fill you with strength to live a life of holiness, a life of God-centeredness, a life of worship. Maybe once upon a time the gospel did great things in your life, but now it no longer moves you. This is a huge problem for anyone who calls themselves a Christian.

In fact, I've even heard it perpetuated in the church that the most intimate season of a Christian's life is when they first understand the gospel. Is that what you believe? Was the gospel exciting only when you first believed it?

I'm not sure where that idea came from, but it is absolutely not true. To stick with my ocean illustration of God's love, the beach is great, the surf is great, but what lies out in the deep is even more magnificent. If your knowledge of the ocean is restricted to what you've experienced on the beach with a Pina Colada in your hand and your feet in the water, you'll never know what the ocean is really like.

Jesus is calling us to leave our comfort, to leave the comfort of the beach, and to swim out into the danger zone. He's not calling us simply for thrills and danger. I'm not saying you need to go to Iraq or something else crazy. I'm saying He's calling us out into the depths of who He is and what He is about. AND, THIS IS NOT SAFE! It is a scary thing to leave the shore behind and swim out into the deep ocean. You might think, "What if

I get tired? What if I lose my way? Who is going to take care of me?" These questions are important, but it's out there, in the deep, where we discover that every single thing we could possibly need has already been given to us in Jesus.

Out there in the wild is where we will come to know Him in a way that we cannot experience on the beach. It takes faith to leave the shore and swim out where the wild things are.

I think this is what the Apostle Paul is talking about in Romans 14:23 when he says, "Whatever does not proceed from faith is sin." Paul is saying our behavior (good and bad) may actually be performed by our own strength and not from faith. I don't know about you, but I can give some money to the poor and not have any faith. I can serve my neighbor and not even think about what Jesus has done for me and how He's motivated my belief. I do it because that's what good people do. But Paul says that is sin because anything that doesn't proceed from faith is sin.

So, what are we to do? Some of us back off and try to play it safe, which keeps us in ankle-deep waters. If you're trying to stay safe, you are not going to experience the danger or the thrill of being out in the deep with God. Your fear and lack of faith will keep you from experiencing the grace of God. Let me put it this way: you cannot learn to swim in ankle-deep water.

God is calling us into a life of faith, and that requires trust. Do you trust Him enough to step into something that you don't quite understand? Maybe it's going to that church down the street and actually joining a small group of people where you can ask questions and grow in your faith. That might sound scary, but maybe that's what God is calling you to do. For you, that is swimming out into the deep, and it is where God will meet you.

Church folk need to hear that too. There's something God has for us that we can't experience in a large Sunday morning gathering. This is one of the reasons why I believe that the only way to make disciples is in community and on mission. The only way to make disciples of Jesus is in the wild! There is something crucial about discipleship that takes place in foreign areas outside the church doors. I'm not talking about foreign mission fields like Africa; I'm talking about your neighborhood and your job. That's where the wild things are. That's where things can get crazy. We have a choice. When Jesus dives into the deep and swims out into the wild, we can decide to go with Him or stay on the shore.

It is out there in community that we really have to deal with our sin. For me this happens when someone asks me a personal question that I don't want to answer, such as asking how well I'm resting, and then reminds me that since Jesus performed perfectly on my behalf (the gospel), I don't need to work seven days a week. Or when somebody's sin rubs me the wrong way and I have to confess and repent of my annoyance or anger. It's easy to pull back from community and mission. All of us, myself included, have a desire in our hearts to pump the brakes and slowly back away from community and mission when things get out of our control. This might happen when you get hurt, or afraid, or the money's coming up short and you start stressing out.

In one of his books, Eugene Peterson says, "Sometimes I think that all religious sites should be posted with signs reading, 'Beware the God.'"[23] What's he saying? Churches are not safe places. Hopefully on a weekly basis you will come into contact with the wild, untamable, uncontrollable, sovereign God; and He's going to mess up your life for good. If you encounter the one true God, He is going to mess up your plans, idol-block you, and call you out of your comfort zone. I know you're scared, but God will meet you out there. Live a life by faith. Live a life that demands a gospel explanation. Go out there in the deep and come face to face with your greatest fears. You may be tempted to think it's the end, but it's just the beginning.

This is hard to say because nobody wants to hear it, but it needs to be said nonetheless.

> God's calling you into a life of faith.
>
> God's calling you to take more risks for the sake of the gospel.
>
> God's calling you to lay your life down and not pick it back up again.
>
> God's calling you to carry your cross and follow Jesus.
>
> God's calling you to sacrifice your comfortable life on the beach for an exhilarating life on Mission with Him out in the deeps.

If you are not a believer in Jesus Christ, I don't want you to hear me saying that going out into the wild is going to make you a Christian. The only way to become a Christian is that someone else already went out into the wild for you, and sacrificed everything for you, and that's Jesus Christ.

The main thing I hope you understand is that Jesus is the true and better Jonah. No one has risked more than Jesus. No one has left the safety of the shore and pushed out into the deep more than Jesus. Jesus willingly left Heaven's shores and came to Earth. That's the wild. Just think about how He came: the all-powerful Son of God whose words created everything. John 1:1-3, 14 tells us that "Jesus is the Word" that spoke galaxies into existence and became flesh. What kind of flesh? A baby. The omnipotent God became a crying baby boy. Jesus was God all-powerful, but He swam out into the deep as a baby, completely entrusting Himself to the Father. That's the obedience of faith.

As a baby, Jesus was powerless. The all-powerful God became powerless. He could have been dropped, starved, and unloved. Jesus completely entrusted Himself to the Father's care. Can you imagine? Theologians call this truth the hypostatic union; He's God and man at the same time. I don't know how that's working out in a baby. Imagine if you were trapped in a baby's body. You would probably be thinking, "Don't drop me right now. You're holding me incorrectly. I need to be burped." I don't know if that's how it was; I doubt it. What I do know is that He was out of control in a sense. He gave Himself up to the Father's control. It was in the wild that Jesus risked literally everything.

But Jesus is more than just a moral example to us. On the cross Jesus became one with us so that we might become one with Him. Jesus took our sin on the cross so that we could take His righteousness. People can't see what Jesus did on the cross without it either melting or hardening their heart. The Puritans used to say, "The same sun that melts the ice hardens the clay."[24]

Some of us don't want a God like that. We want to be good enough. We don't want to be reminded of how broken we are. Every time we look to the cross, we're reminded we can't save ourselves. However, at the cross we're also reminded of how deeply we are loved. Jesus loved us so much that He willingly pushed out into the deep for us. If you're a Christian, you cannot think about what Jesus has done for you and then stay on the beach.

I'm not saying it is easy. I realize that it's tough. In fact, it's more than tough; it's impossible without an ongoing awareness of the grace of God in community and on mission with Jesus. That's one of the reasons it is so important to gather with believers each week. That's one of the reasons we should celebrate the Lord's Supper regularly. We need to be reminded constantly of how far Jesus was willing to go to save us.

It's my prayer that you would put your faith and trust in Jesus Christ, find a good, gospel-centered church in your town, and follow Jesus out into the deep for the rest of your life. If you need some help finding such a church, you can start here: http://www.acts29.com/find-churches/.

ENDNOTES

1. C.S. Lewis, *Surprised by Joy* (Orlando: Harcourt, 1955), 227.
2. Timothy Keller, "Covenant Love" (sermon, August 16, 2009), sourced from Logos Bible Software.
3. Herman Melville, *Moby Dick* (Boston: C. H. Simonds Co., 1892), 44.
4. Elvis Mitchell, "Shia Labeouf," *Interview*, accessed October 19, 2015, http://www. interviewmagazine.com/film/shia-labeouf#_.
5. Ibid.
6. Keller, "A New Humanity" (sermon, November 6, 2011), sourced from Logos Bible Software.
7. Keller, "They Greatly Feared" (sermon, September 23, 2001), sourced from Logos Bible Software.
8. Ambrose John Wilson, ased Sign of the Prophet Jonah and Its Modern Confirmations,ah*The Princeton Theological Review* 25, no. 4 (1927): 640, accessed October 19, 2015, http:// journals.ptsem.edu/id/ BR1927254/dmd005.

9. Richard Foster, quoted in O. Hallesby, *Prayer: A World Famous Classic to Deepen and Enrich Your Prayer Life* (Minneapolis: Augsburg Fortress, 1994), 23.

10. O. Hallesby, *Prayer: A World Famous Classic to Deepen and Enrich Your Prayer Life* (Minneapolis: Augsburg Fortress, 1994), 18.

11. Paul Miller, *A Praying Life: Connecting with God in a Distracting World* (Colorado Springs: NavPress, 2009), 29.

12. Ibid., 49.

13. A. W. Tozer, *The Knowledge of the Holy* (New York: HarperOne, 1961), 1.

14. R.C. Sproul, *Reason to Believe* (Grand Rapids: Zondervan, 1982), 29.

15. Alan Redpath, quoted in Charles R. Swindoll, *Saying It Well: Touching Others with Your Words* (New York: Faith Words, 2012).

16. Timothy Keller, "Faith Rising" (sermon, August 12, 1990), sourced from Logos Bible Software.

17. Timothy Keller, "The Secret Siege of Nineveh" (sermon, August 26, 1990), sourced from Logos Bible Software.

18. John Calvin, *Institutes of the Christian Religion*, trans. Henry Beveridge (Peabody, WA: Hendrickson Publishers, Inc., 2008), 55.

19. Christopher J. H. Wright, *The Mission of God* (Downers Grove, IL: InterVarsity Press, 2006), 169.

20. C.S. Lewis, *The Lion, the Witch and the Wardrobe* (New York: Harper Collins, 1950), 80.

21. David F. Wells, *God in the Wasteland: The Reality of Truth in*

a World of Fading Dreams (Grand Rapids: Wm. B. Eerdmans Publishing Co., 1994), 114.

22. G. K. Chesterton, *Orthodoxy* (New York, John Lane Co., 1908), 108.

23. Eugene Peterson, *Leap over a Wall: Earthy Spirituality for Everyday Christians* (New York: HarperOne, 1998), 144.

24. Puritan saying, quoted in Matt Chandler, *The Explicit Gospel* (Wheaton, IL: Crossway, 2012), 68.

p. 34 Return of Christ. Look busy!

CPSIA information can be obtained at www.ICGtesting.com
Printed in the USA
BVOW08s1254020116

431505BV00003B/94/P

9 781632 960627